CAN THERE BE PEACE BETWEEN

JEWS AND ARABS?

THE BIBLICAL AND ISLAMIC PERSPECTIVE

FAROOQ MIRZA

From
The Quran Foundation

ISBN: 978-1-80558-707-1 (Paperback)
ISBN: 978-1-80558-708-8 (Hardcover)

All rights reserved. Copyright © 2025 by Farooq Mirza,
No part of this publication may be reproduced for commercial purposes, stored in a retrieval system, or transmitted in any form or by any means, electronic, mechanical, photocopying, recording, or otherwise, without the author's written permission.

CONTENTS

Summary Of The Document 1

The Origin Of Arab Israeli Dispute 3

    Chapter 1 The Covenant With Abraham A Study Of Its Significance And Legacy 4

    Chapter 2 The Promise Of Ishmael 9

    Chapter 3 The Three Key Patriarchs: Abraham, Isaac, And Jacob 14

    Chapter 4 Did God Renege His Promise To Ishmael? 18

    Chapter 5 The Eviction Of Hagar And Ishmael 25

Ideological Conflict Between Prophet Muhammad And The Jews 32

    Chapter 6 Prophet Muhammad Contact With The Jews 33

    Chapter 7 Islam: A Continuation Of Abraham's Monotheism 41

    Chapter 8 God's Chosen People 45

    Chapter 9 The Quran's Critique Of Jewish Non-Compliance 49

War Between Prophet Muhammad And The Jews 55

    Chapter 10 The Expulsion Of Banu Qaynuqa: Fact Or Fiction? 56

    Chapter 11 The Treachery Of Banu Al-Nadir 59

    Chapter 12 The Banu Qurayzah Massacre: Fact Or Fiction? 62

    Chapter 13 War Against The Jews Of Khaybar 67

Call For Unity And Peace 71

    Chapter 14 A Case For Jewish Homeland The History Of The Persecution Of Jews 72

Chapter 15 Islamophobia Its Origins, Impact, And
Future Challenges 82

Chapter 16 The Divine Law Of Diversity 86

Chapter 17 Common Beliefs Among Jews, Christians,
And Muslims 90

Chapter 18 What Did Jesus Say About Salvation? 94

Chapter 19 The Universal Doctrine Of Salvation 98

Chapter 20 The Two Nation Theory? 105

Chapter 21 The Vision Of Unity 108

SUMMARY OF THE DOCUMENT

The document explores the historical, theological, and cultural aspects of the relationship between Jews and Arabs, focusing on biblical and Islamic perspectives. It delves into the origins of the Arab-Israeli dispute, the ideological and military conflicts between Prophet Muhammad and Jewish tribes, and the call for unity and peace among Abrahamic faiths.

- **Origins of the Arab-Israeli Dispute**: The document examines the covenant with Abraham, the promise of Ishmael, and the birth of Isaac, highlighting the significance of these events in the context of the Arab-Israeli conflict.
- **War Between Prophet Muhammad and the Jews**: The document details the military confrontations between Prophet Muhammad and the Jewish tribes, including the expulsion of Banu Qaynuqa, the treachery of Banu al-Nadir, and the massacre of Banu Qurayzah.
- **Jewish Persecution Under Islam**: The document contrasts the persecution of Jews under Islam with that under Christianity, noting periods of relative stability and cultural flourishing in Islamic lands.
- **Understanding Antisemitism**: The origins and expressions of antisemitism in Christian and Islamic contexts are examined, emphasizing the need for dismantling prejudices to achieve equitable coexistence.
- **Islamophobia**: The document explores the origins, impact, and future challenges of Islamophobia, highlighting its historical roots and contemporary manifestations.
- **Divine Law of Diversity**: The principle of diversity as an intrinsic element of divine intention is discussed, emphasizing the adaptability of God's will to various audiences throughout history.

- **Common Beliefs Among Abrahamic Faiths:** The shared beliefs among Judaism, Christianity, and Islam are highlighted, focusing on the oneness of God, shared prophetic traditions, and the sanctity of places of worship.
- **Call for Unity and Peace:** The call for unity and peace among Jews, Christians, and Muslims is emphasized, highlighting common beliefs and the shared heritage of the Abrahamic faiths.

THE ORIGIN OF ARAB ISRAELI DISPUTE

CHAPTER 1

THE COVENANT WITH ABRAHAM A STUDY OF ITS SIGNIFICANCE AND LEGACY

This chapter delves into the covenant between God and Abraham, which is foundational for Judaism, Christianity, and Islam. It explores three essential promises made to Abraham: land, descendants, and blessings for all nations. The chapter highlights Abraham's journey from polytheism to monotheism, emphasizing his unwavering faith and inner strength. This chapter will explore these key components of the Abrahamic covenant, and the historical context of deception in Egypt, and analyze the implications of the narratives surrounding Ishmael and his descendants, ultimately shedding light on the enduring significance of these stories in religious discourse.

Abraham, a foundational figure

Abraham's portrayal in the Bible and the Quran encapsulates spiritual growth and moral clarity. Through his journey from polytheism to monotheism, dialogues with authority figures, and his ultimate rejection of falsehood, Abraham emerges as an exemplar of unwavering faith and inner strength. His life lessons resonate through the ages, encouraging a return to belief in a singular God but also inspiring critical thought against blind adherence to tradition. Abraham represents not only a prophet but also a foundational figure. His legacy is defined by devotion, reasoning, and the pursuit of truth. In emulating him, believers are called to reflect on their beliefs and cultivate a deep, personal understanding of their faith.

The Original Covenant

The covenant between God and Abraham stands out as a fundamental compact for multiple faith traditions, including Judaism, Christianity, and Islam. The original covenant bestowed upon Abraham is intricately tied to his identity and legacy. It is established through three essential promises: the promise of land, the promise of descendants, and the blessing that flows through him to all nations.

A) The promise of land

A) The Lord said to Abraham, "Go from your country, your people and your father's household to the land [Canaan] I will show you." (Gen 12:1) The first part of the covenant is the promise of land, articulated when God commands Abraham to leave his homeland: "Go from your country to the land I will show you." This directive not only establishes a physical territory but also frames Abraham's journey of faith as he steps into the unknown, relying on divine guidance. As the narrative progresses, Canaan is identified as a promised land. "The *whole land of Canaan, where you now reside as a foreigner, I will give as an everlasting possession to you and your descendants after you, and I will be their God." Then God said to Abraham, "As for you, you must keep my covenant, you and your descendants after you for the generations to come. (Genesis 17:8)* All this was predicated upon the descendants of Abraham to honor their end of the bargain by keeping the covenant.

B) The Promise of Descendants

"I will make you into a mighty nation, and I will bless you." (Gen 12:2) The second element of the covenant centers on descendants. Throughout the narrative, the theme of progeny is emphasized, marking Abraham as the patriarch of a people destined to grow into a multitude. As the narrative progresses, about the promise of descendants when the Lord affirms that *"I will make your offspring like the dust of the earth." (Gen 13:16)* The scope of Abraham's legacy expands to encompass countless

nations. *"I will transform you into a mighty nation." (12:2) "I will make your offspring like the dust of the earth so that if anyone could count the dust, your offspring could be numbered." (Gen 13:16) "Look up at the sky and count the stars—if indeed you can count them." Then the Lord spoke to him, "So shall your offspring be." (Gen 15:5) When Abram was ninety-nine years old, the Lord appeared to him and said, "I will make my covenant between me and you and will greatly increase your numbers. You will be the father of many nations. I will make you very fruitful and kings will come from you. I will establish my covenant as an everlasting covenant between me and you and your descendants after you for generations to come. I will be your God and the God of your descendants after you."* (Genesis 17:1-7).

The second part of the original covenant is known as the descendants' promise. This is where God promised Abraham that I would greatly increase your numbers and make you into nations. This was when God changed Abram's name to Abraham, meaning 'father of many nations.' The mention of Abraham's descendants was general. The earth's dust represents Abraham's uncountable offspring. Similar phrases like "as numerous as the stars in the sky" and "as the sand on the seashore" represent Abraham's progeny. (Genesis 15:5, 22:17, 28:14).

Innumerable Descendants Include Who?

God promised Abraham that his descendants would be as numerous as the dust of the earth, illustrating their uncountable nature. This promise is reiterated through various metaphors, likening Abraham's progeny to the stars in the sky and the sand on the seashore. However, the implications of this include a demographic reality that transcends the Jewish population, which, as of recent estimates, is around 15 million - too small to justify the above description of innumerable Abraham's offspring. When considering the broader context of Abraham's offspring, including Arabs and Muslims, as well as Christians, the figure swells into the billions. This suggests a fulfillment of the promise of diverse populations across nations. When

Abraham's offspring from his three wives are added, one can almost compare them with countless Abraham's descendants. This intertwining of faith and ancestry speaks to Abraham's global legacy as a monotheistic figure, uniting diverse peoples under a shared heritage.

C) Universal Blessings through Abraham

"I will make your name great, and you will be a blessing. ***All peoples on earth will be blessed through you.****" (Gen 12:4)* The third component, perhaps the most profound, is the universal promise of blessing. This promise positions Abraham not just as a recipient of God's favor but as a conduit of divine blessing for all humanity. This indicates the far-reaching implications of this covenant.

In **Judaism**, it signifies identity formation, a strong connection to heritage, and the assurance of a collective promise given by God. This reaffirms their status as chosen people to carry out the message of Abraham's monotheism to the rest of the world. This identity is vital in shaping Jewish religious practice, communal life, and resilience in the face of historical persecution.

In **Christianity**, the covenant is viewed as a precursor to the New Covenant brought by Jesus Christ. Believers are invited to join Abraham's family through faith. The New Testament elaborates on this by emphasizing that "if you belong to Christ, you are Abraham's seed, and heirs according to the promise" (Galatians 3:29). This perspective fosters inclusivity, suggesting that the covenant blessings are accessible to all who believe in Christ, regardless of ethnicity or background.

For Muslims, the covenant invokes a sense of belonging to a lineage that encompasses a galaxy of prophets and interfaith connections. Islam honors Abraham as a prophet and the father of many nations, affirming the covenant's relevance through its teachings in the Quran.

This recognition of shared ancestry emphasizes the universality of God's message and invites Muslims to engage in compassionate dialogue with the "People of the Book."

CHAPTER 2

THE PROMISE OF ISHMAEL

This chapter continues the theme of the second part of the covenant: innumerable Abraham's descendants. It explores the story of Ishmael, Abraham's first son, and the promises made to him. It begins with the acquisition of Hagar from Egypt, who became Ishmael's mother. The chapter discusses the moral complexities of Abraham and Sarah's actions, including Sarah giving Hagar to Abraham to bear a child. It highlights the angel's announcement of Ishmael's birth. It also promises that Ishmael will have numerous descendants fulfilling God's covenant with Abraham. The chapter also describes Ishmael's contrasting portrayals in biblical and Samaritan texts. The former depicts him as a "wild donkey of a man" and the latter offers a more positive characterization. The narrative examines the implications of these portrayals for modern perceptions of Arab identity, Islamophobia, and relations among Abrahamic faiths.

Acquisition of Hagar from Egypt

Upon arriving in Canaan, Abraham and Sarah faced famine, prompting them to migrate to Egypt. Here, a moment of moral failure arises when Abraham instructs Sarah to pose as his sister to safeguard his life: "When the Egyptians see you are a beautiful woman, they will say, 'This is his wife.' Then they will kill me, but let you live." (Abraham was telling a partial truth because Sarah was his half-sister.) This deception, while rooted in fear, illustrates the complex nature of faith and obedience as Abraham attempts to navigate perilous circumstances using worldly tactics. Ultimately, Sarah is taken into Pharaoh's household. God intervenes, afflicting Pharaoh's house with plagues until the truth is revealed. Despite their deception, it is Pharaoh who suffers divine wrath. Sarah's return to Abraham was accompanied by gifts from Pharaoh, including slave girl Hagar. Abraham acquired considerable wealth and returned to Canaan.

This story is shocking from a Muslim perspective, where prophets are fallible humans but also not guilty of major moral sins. What is the difference between a prophet and an ordinary sinner? Abraham in fact traded his wife for gifts from the Pharaoh. Sarah did not object to this trade either. Pharaoh an evil man seemed to have more moral sense than Abraham. At least, he generously rewarded Abraham who became rich with silver, gold, and cattle. This blasphemous story is not mentioned in the Quran.

The Promise of a Son and Ishmael's Conception

Abram said to the Lord, "You have given me no children, so a servant in my household will be my heir." Then the word of the Lord came to him: "This man (Abraham's servant) will not be your heir, but a son who is your own flesh and blood will be your heir." (Gen 15:1-4)

Frustrated by her barrenness, Sarah gave Hagar to Abraham to bear a child to fulfill a divine plan. *"Sarah took her Egyptian slave Hagar and gave her to Abraham to be his wife. He slept with Hagar, and she conceived (with Ishmael). When Hagar knew she was pregnant, she despised her mistress. Sarah mistreated Hagar so much that she fled from her." (Gen 16:3-6)*

Angel's Announcement of the Birth of Ishmael

The angel intercepted Hagar and told her to "return to your mistress and submit to her authority." The angel also told her, "I will greatly multiply your descendants, too many to count." Behold, you are pregnant and will give birth to a son, and you shall name him Ishmael because the Lord has heard your affliction." (Gen 16:9-11) Out of the twelve Biblical personalities, Ishmael was honored, for God chose his name. Ishmael means "God listens," in this case, to Hagar's plea for help while she wandered homeless, helpless, and afraid.

A Wild Donkey of a Man: Ishmael's Characterization

Angel continued: "*But he (Ishmael) will be a wild donkey of a man. His hand will be against everyone, and everyone's hand will be against him, and he will live in defiance of all his brothers.*" (Gen 16:12) "*Abraham was eighty-six years old when Hagar bore Ishmael to him.*" (Gen 16:15-16)

The biblical account depicts Ishmael in contrasting lights. Upon being named by the angel, "Ishmael," meaning "God hears," signifies divine compassion towards Hagar. However, this is juxtaposed with the prophecy that Ishmael would be "a wild donkey of a man," indicating a life marked by conflict and violence. This characterization is the first step in the series of denigrating depictions of Ishmael in the Bible. It raises crucial questions about the biblical text's motives. As the narrative unfolds, it suggests that the perception of Ishmael—and implicitly his descendants—was shaped in a way that justified Isaac's status as the favored son. Historical and rabbinic interpretations often lean towards disparaging characterizations of Ishmael. It contributes to stereotypes of Arab populations as violent or chaotic. Such misrepresentations have significant ramifications, fostering prejudice and misunderstanding within Judeo-Christian contexts. Biblical apologists downplay this by saying Ishmael would become independent like a wild donkey. The fact is that this is the first step in an attempt at denigration of Ishmael's character but also an implicit accusation against his descendants (Arabs), portrayed as a violent and brutal race.

The interpretative divergences surrounding Ishmael's character have profound implications for how descendants of these biblical figures are viewed today. This is especially true for Arabs and Muslims. From the declaration of abundant descendants to the characterization of Ishmael as "a wild donkey of a man," the biblical texts provide a negative analysis that affects modern perceptions of Arab identity and relations among Abrahamic faiths.

Imagine the psychological trauma Hagar suffered. She is lonely, homeless, and on the run. Now, she is told she will be the mother of mayhem, and a monster is growing inside her. What was the purpose of such a crude and cruel prediction? Did this prediction prove true? The Bible provides no evidence for Ishmael's violent behavior. It was not Ishmael's descendants who committed the Holocaust.

Alternative Perspectives: The Samaritan Torah

The Samaritan Pentateuch, also known as the Samaritan Torah, is the text of the first five books of the Hebrew Bible written in Samaritan script. *"He [Ishmael] will be fertile. His hand will be with everyone, and everyone's hand will be with him, and he will live among all his brothers."* The Samaritan Torah offers an intriguing counter-narrative to the traditional view found in the Masoretic Text. Here, Ishmael is described positively as "a fertile man," with a harmonious relationship with others. Being fertile, Ishmael fulfilled Abraham's "descendants' covenant." This description contrasts sharply with the negative portrayal in the Hebrew version, suggesting a dialectic between how different communities understand Ishmael's legacy. By emphasizing fertility and cooperation, the Samaritan account aligns with a more inclusive vision of community. This stands in stark contrast to the divisive narrative found in the dominant Jewish and Christian texts.

Furthermore, the narrative illustrates the enduring concept of divine election. Ishmael is recognized as a significant figure among Abraham's children despite the complicated dynamics of his birth. This acknowledgment speaks to the broader theological assertion that God's covenant extends beyond Isaac's physical lineage, reinforcing the notion that all believers can trace their spiritual heritage to Abraham.

(Samaritans emerged as a distinct group following the Assyrian conquest. Their identity reflects the complex interactions between Jewish and non-Jewish populations.)

Ishmael's identity is heavily contested in the biblical narrative. The angelic proclamation that he would be "a wild donkey of a man" (Gen 16:12) has been interpreted variously; many view it as a denigration intended to establish a dichotomy between Ishmael's descendants and those of Isaac. Critics argue that this character assessment perpetuates negative stereotypes about Arabs and Muslims. Conversely, the Samaritan Torah offers a more favorable depiction, stating that Ishmael would be "fertile" and live "among all his brothers," painting him in a positive light and contributing to an understanding of Abraham's descendants' shared lineage and legacy.

CHAPTER 3

THE THREE KEY PATRIARCHS: ABRAHAM, ISAAC, AND JACOB

THE PROMISE OF ISAAC

This chapter delves into the Quranic depiction of the three key patriarchs: Abraham, Isaac, and Jacob. It highlights the Quran's emphasis on their roles as prophets and their significance in the Islamic faith. The chapter explores how the Quran portrays Abraham as a model of unwavering faith and obedience to God. It emphasizes his monotheistic beliefs and rejection of idolatry. It also discusses the Quranic narrative of Isaac and Jacob, focusing on their roles as prophets and contributions to the Abrahamic legacy. The Quran's portrayal of these patriarchs as exemplars of faith, unity, and shared heritage among Jews, Christians, and Muslims.

Abraham, Isaac, and Jacob in the Quran

And after he [Abraham] withdrew from them [his homeland, Iraq] and from all, they worshipped instead of God. We bestowed upon him (Abraham) Isaac and Jacob and made each a prophet. We bestowed upon them [manifold] gifts out of Our grace and granted them a lofty power to convey the truth [to others]. (Quran 19:49-50) [As for Abraham], We blessed Isaac and [Isaac's son] Jacob upon him and caused prophethood and revelation to continue among his offspring. And We gave him his reward in this world, and in life to come. He shall find himself among the righteous. (Quran 29:27) And call to mind Our servants Abraham, Isaac, and Jacob, [all of them] endowed with inner strength and vision: for, verily, We purified them by means of thought the purest: the remembrance of life to come. And behold, in Our sight, they were indeed among the elect, the truly righteous! (Quran 38:45-47)

Birth of Isaac in the Bible

Isaac's birth and its significance in the biblical narrative begins with God's promise to Abraham and Sarah that they would have a son despite their advanced age. God's promise to Abraham regarding Isaac's birth is a pivotal moment in the biblical narrative.

God said to Abraham, "I will bless her (Sarah) and will surely give you a son from her. She will be the mother of nations; kings of peoples will come from her." Abraham laughed and said to himself, "Will a son be born to a man a hundred years old? Will Sarah bear a child at ninety?" (Genesis 17:15-16).

The Quranic Version of Isaac's Birth

In the Quran, angels deliver the good news of Isaac's impending birth to Abraham and Sarah. The angel, *"Gave him [Abraham] the glad tidings of [the birth of] a son who would be endowed with deep knowledge." (Quran 51:28)* "*His wife (Sarah), standing nearby, laughed. Thereupon, We gave her the glad tiding of [the birth of] Isaac and, after Isaac, of [his son] Jacob." Said she: "Oh, woe is me! Shall I bear a child now that I am an old woman, and this husband is an older man?" (Quran 11:71-72)* Sarah's disbelief, who viewed the revelation as implausible due to their advanced age, highlighted the miraculous nature of God's decrees that challenge human understanding. Abraham's question regarding the certainty of this promise further emphasizes faith in the divine will. He grappled with doubt despite his foundational belief.

Jacob's Inheritance and Prophetic Role

Isaac's son Jacob inherited not only the covenant but also a new identity—Israel—a name that resonates through history as synonymous with the Jewish people and their homeland. Jacob's story underscores familial faith and devotion. When death approached Jacob, he said to his sons: *"Whom will you worship after I am gone?" They answered: "We will worship thy God, the God of thy forefathers Abraham,*

Ishmael, and Isaac, the One God; and unto Him will we surrender ourselves." (Quran 2:133) In his last moments, Jacob ensured that his sons would remain steadfast in their worship of the One God, voicing his concerns about their adherence to the covenant established by their patriarchs. This act exemplifies the transference of faith and the significance of maintaining religious identity across generations. Jacob's admonitions to his sons highlight the imperative nature of his lineage's adherence to the covenant. When presented with the notion of their future worship, Jacob's words served as an echo of Abraham's legacy: the importance of submission to God, a theme that resonates deeply within Jewish thought and practice.

Joseph

Biblically, Jacob had four wives: Leah, Rachel, and two slave girls. Leah and Rachel were sisters and Jacob's first cousins. Jacob fathered twelve sons, who became leaders of Israel's twelve tribes. One of them was Joseph, a key figure in the Old Testament and the Quran. (The Quran's chapter 12 is devoted to Joseph and his trials and tribulations) Joseph and Benjamin were full brothers, sons of Jacob's wife Rachel, whereas the other ten were half-brothers. Joseph's mother, Rachel, died while giving birth to Benjamin.

Joseph was Jacob's favorite son, and his half-brothers envied him. They took Joseph out into the wilderness and threw him in a shallow well. According to the Bible (Genesis 37:25), the caravan of "Ishmaelites", or Arabs, "came from Gilead with their camels bearing spice and balm and myrrh, carrying it down to Egypt." Gilead is the Biblical name for the region east of Jordan. They discovered Joseph in the well, took him to Egypt with them, and sold him into slavery.

The Origins of the Hebrews in Egypt

In Egypt, Joseph's descendants were fruitful and their numbers increased significantly. They enjoyed prosperity and honor for a few generations. There arose a king in Egypt, and he said the people of Israel were too many. Egyptians feared Jews might join foreign invaders (Exodus 1:10). Previously, the alien Hyksos dynasty invaded Egypt and allied with the Hebrews. To protect themselves from this danger, they decided to have every male Hebrew child killed, as stated in the Quran and the Bible. Then, the Egyptian dynasty dispossessed them of their wealth and reduced them to slavery, from which Moses freed them. The Hebrew prophet, teacher, leader, lawgiver, and warrior, Moshe, or Moses, delivered his people from Egyptian slavery. Moses is the most frequently mentioned prophet in the Quran. His life story is mentioned in twenty-five chapters, and his name is cited 136 times in the Quran. The story of the Israelites being freed from Pharaoh's bonds inspired Muslims of Mecca undergoing suffering in a pagan society.

The Duality of Righteousness and Sin Among Israelites

Isaac and Jacob's narratives contain essential lessons about righteousness and humanity. The Quran makes clear that, despite divine blessings bestowed upon Abraham, Isaac, and Jacob, their descendants embody both virtuous and sinful behavior. *"Among the offspring of these two were [destined] to be both doers of good and would glaringly sin against themselves." (Quran 37:113)* This duality serves as a reminder that God's election of a people does not equate to inherent superiority or exemption from moral responsibility but rather emphasizes the need for continual faithfulness and commitment to God's path.

CHAPTER 4

DID GOD RENEGE HIS PROMISE TO ISHMAEL?

The chapter explores the implications of Isaac being considered the "only seed of Abraham," highlighting the distinction between Isaac and Abraham's other children, including Ishmael. It addresses the perceived superiority of Isaac's descendants, particularly Jacob's sons, and the lasting impact of these beliefs on Jewish-Arab relations.

God's Covenant with Isaac Only

When God promised Abraham that Sarah would have a son, Abraham felt this was almost too much to expect, given his and Sarah's old age. Abraham was perfectly content with Ishmael as an heir to the covenant promise: Abraham said to God, *"If only Ishmael might live under your blessing!" Then God said, "Yes, but your wife Sarah will bear you a son, and you will call him Isaac. I will establish my covenant with him as an everlasting covenant for his descendants after him. And as for Ishmael, I surely bless him; I will make him fruitful and will greatly increase his numbers. He will be the father of twelve rulers, and I will make him into a great nation.* **But my covenant I will establish with Isaac,** *whom Sarah will bear to you by this time next year." (Genesis 17:18-21)*

This promise of Isaac comes amidst Abraham's concerns and desires for Ishmael, his firstborn son. However, God distinctly affirms that His covenant will be established through Isaac, whom Sarah will bear. This situation prompts fundamental questions regarding the interpretation of Abraham's seed, the divine choice, and the ensuing narrative of inheritance and covenant. Thus, Abraham's second son,

Isaac, and his descendants were **"chosen"** as **"the only seed of Abraham."** Ishmael would have a notable line of descendants.

The Meaning of Only Abraham's Seed

At the heart of the discourse on Abraham's seed lies the definition and implications of that seed. Abraham, who had children with three women—Sarai (Sarah), Hagar, and Keturah—fathered multiple sons: Ishmael, Isaac, and the sons of Keturah. While from a biological perspective, all these children are Abraham's seed, the biblical text grants unique significance to Isaac as the child of promise, where Jews and Christians traditionally assert that the covenant established by God is exclusive to Isaac's lineage, thereby excluding Ishmael. Here the Quran and the Bible part company.

Ishmael Biracial Child of a Black Concubine

Ishmael was a biracial child born to an African concubine, thus racially inferior to Isaac, who belonged to Abraham and Sarah's superior tribe. Isaac's racial purity elevates him among his siblings to be worthy of being the "only seed or heir of Abraham." Isaac's descendants were declared "the chosen people." This means the entire wealth of Abraham, including the land of Canaan belonged only to Isaac, and the other sons were excluded. It gave rise to the Jewish demand that the land of Canaan belonged only to the "seed of Abraham" and that Arabs had no right to live on this land.

The Superiority of Jacob's Sons

The following biblical verses establish Isaac, Jacob, and their descendants' racial superiority. When Isaac blessed Jacob, he told him: *"May nations serve you and peoples bow down to you. Be lord over your brothers and may your mother's sons bow down to you. May those who curse you be cursed and those who bless you be blessed." (Gen.27:29)* These nations are the offspring of Ishmael and Keturah (Gen. Rabbah 66:4). The Rabbis stress that the subjugation of Keturah's children to Israel is eternal. The supposed racial superiority of Jews over Arabs is the foundation of modern Israel, described as an apartheid state by human rights organizations.

Denial of Ishmael's Paternity

In the famous verse of Abraham's son's sacrifice, Isaac was declared the only son, meaning the only seed of Abraham marginalizing Ishmael within the Abrahamic family. *"And God said, take now thy son,* **your only son Isaac,** *whom thou lovest, and bring thee into the land of Moriah. (Genesis 22:2)*
To a casual reader, it may appear as a typographical error that the scribe forgot that Abraham had two sons. This was an insidious move to sanctify Isaac as Abraham's only seed and further denigrate Ishmael. God's instruction to take **"your only son Isaac"** reinforces the narrative that Isaac is viewed as the singular heir. This phrase not only diminishes Ishmael's role but also sanctifies Isaac's status as the sole progeny through which the promises are to be realized. This theological framing has permitted interpretations that legitimize the Jewish exclusive claim to the land of Canaan while also marginalizing Ishmael's descendants despite their foundational connection to Abraham.

The Story of Sacrifice Quranic Version

And [one Day], when [the child] became old enough to share in his [father's] endeavors, the latter said: "O my dear son! I have seen in a dream that I should sacrifice you. Consider, then, what would be your view?" [Abraham's son] answered: "O my father! Do as you are bidden. You will find me, if Allah so wills, among those who are patient in adversity!" But as soon as the two had surrendered themselves to [what they believed] the will of Allah, and [Abraham] had laid him down on his face, We called out to him: "O Abraham and you have already fulfilled [the purpose of] that dream-vision!" (37:102–105)

There is no mention of either Ishmael or Isaac in the verses above. Yet if Isaac was offered as a sacrifice, Muslims would still celebrate this event with the same enthusiasm because Ishmael and Isaac were prophets of God, according to the Holy Quran.

BROKEN PROMISES

From the biblical description, God reneged on His promises to Ishmael soon after Isaac's birth. Circumcision is the seal of an ***everlasting*** covenant. However, soon after Isaac's birth, God supposedly broke the everlasting covenant with Ishmael and made an exclusive covenant with Isaac.

Circumcision is the Covenant Seal

"Males among you shall be circumcised. It will be the sign of a covenant between me and you. For generations to come, every male among you who is eight days old must be circumcised, including those born in your household. **My covenant in your flesh is to be an everlasting covenant.** *Any uncircumcised male, who has not been circumcised in the flesh, will be cut off from his people." (Genesis 17:10-14) "Abraham was ninety-nine years old when he was circumcised, and his son Ishmael was thirteen; Abraham and Ishmael were circumcised on that very day. (Genesis 17:24-26)*

The seal of God's covenant was circumcision. Abraham and Ishmael were circumcised on the same day. The command of circumcision establishes a physical sign of God's promise. It represents both a cutting—a severing of the individual from the surrounding cultures—and an initiation into a sacred community defined by faith and obedience. The cutting away of the foreskin of the flesh denotes God's promise to cut off covenant breakers from His presence, His people, and His blessing. The act embodies God's everlasting commitment to Abraham and his descendants while highlighting membership in the covenant community. This is a defining ritual for both Jewish and

Muslim communities, marking their heritage and faithfulness to a higher divine.

Everlasting covenant

For thirteen years, Ishmael was Abraham's sole heir and was part of the everlasting covenant through circumcision. However, with Isaac's birth, Ishmael was no longer under the covenant, and all the promises were broken. As a teenager, Ishmael endured a painful circumcision, symbolically establishing an everlasting covenant with God. Muslim boys are circumcised today, following Ishmael and Abraham's tradition.

Law of primogeniture

Primogeniture was a widespread institution in ancient Israelite society. The firstborn son receives a double inheritance portion. Bestowing all the wealth to Isaac violates the laws of primogeniture described in Deuteronomy 21:16, which states that if a man has two wives and the firstborn son is from the wife he doesn't love, he must give the firstborn son twice as much share of his property. Ishmael according to the law of primogeniture should have received double Isaac's share, instead he was banished into the desert.

Immutability of the Divine

Did God renege on His promise? The notion of divine immutability holds theological significance in discussions about God's promises. One of God's attributes is "He never changes" or "immutable." Thus, it is challenging to reconcile the theological assertion that God "reneged" on His affirmation of Ishmael.

Selective interpretation of Scripture

The assertion that Ishmael falls outside the covenantal promise reflects a prejudice that values racial purity over biological connection. This prejudice posits Isaac as the singular heir to Abraham's covenant. The perception that Ishmael's line is rejected through a selective interpretation of scripture opens a significant dialogue about the sanctity and integrity of the textual tradition. The Quran and the Bible offer differing narratives on this issue, raising questions about authorship and distortion. The Quran emphasizes the dual inclusion of Ishmael and Isaac in the covenantal promise. This suggests that divine intention extends beyond Isaac's lineage. The implications of this are profound as they challenge exclusivity and call into question traditionally marginalized Ishmael descendants.

Altering the Scripture

Woe unto those who write down, with their own hands, [something they claim to be] divine writ. They then say, "This is from God," gaining a trifling gain. Woe unto them for what their hands have written, and woe unto them for all they may have gained! (Quran 2:79)

The reference here is to the scholars responsible for misinterpreting the Bible text and misleading their ignorant followers. The "trifling gain" is their feeling of pre-eminence as the alleged "chosen people" because of their descent from Abraham. In the gospel, according to St. Luke in the New Testament, chapter 3, verse 8, John the Baptist condemned the concept of chosen people. "Bring forth, therefore, fruits worthy of repentance, and do not say within yourselves, we have Abraham our father: for I say unto you, that God is able of these stones to raise up children unto Abraham."

Conclusion

The birth of Isaac as the only seed of Abraham encapsulates themes of biased human interpretation and faulty theological assertion. The selective understanding of scripture has contributed to the historical tension between Isaac and Ishmael's descendants. The construction of chosen people and the marginalization of those perceived as outside that chosen lineage is the root cause of tension. The challenge remains to reconcile these historical narratives with an understanding of divine inclusivity and the broader scope of God's promises. These promises transcend human limitations and interpretations. The Islamic narrative extends the promise of blessings to both Isaac and Ishmael. It maintains that Abraham's descendants encompass not only the Jewish people but also the Arab nations linked to Ishmael

CHAPTER 5

THE EVICTION OF HAGAR AND ISHMAEL

The account of Hagar and Ishmael's expulsion from Abraham's household stands as a pivotal event in both Judeo-Christian and Islamic narratives, serving as a foundation for the ongoing complexities in the relationships between Jews and Arabs. The biblical account in Genesis presents a stark depiction of familial conflict influenced by jealousy and entitlement. The Quran does not mention the expulsion of Hagar and Ishmael. The Arabian narrative based on hadith and tradition offers a different narrative filled with compassion and divine intervention.

The Biblical Narrative of Expulsion

The series of denigrating depictions of Ishmael in the Bible suggests that the perception of Ishmael—and implicitly his descendants—was shaped in a way that justified Isaac's status as the favored son. In the final act of cruelty, Ishmael and his mother were evicted and abandoned in the desert to certain death. They were saved only by a literal miracle.

But Sarah saw that the son of Hagar the Egyptian had borne to Abraham was mocking. She said to Abraham, "Get rid of that slave woman and her son, for that woman's son will never share in the inheritance with my son Isaac." (Gen 21:9-10)

Sarah's statement made abundantly clear that the motivation for evicting Ishmael was greed so that Isaac could inherit all of Abraham's estate. It was a manifestation of covenant privilege. This ultimately led to Ishmael's suffering (Genesis 21:8-21). The familial bonds were severed due to greed and the exclusive nature of Isaac's covenant. Hagar and Ishmael were sent away with only scant provisions to certain death. This led Hagar to despair as she attempted to protect her son from death by dehydration in the wilderness. The account highlights the psychological complexities of Sarah's character. It illustrates how her assumed superiority and entitlement directly result in profound suffering for Hagar and Ishmael. Sarah's status as the "chosen" matriarch compels Abraham to act against his better judgment, expelling those he loves in favor of preserving cruel societal norms.

The Arabian Legend and Divine Mercy

In stark contrast, the Islamic tradition, as articulated through various hadiths and narratives, presents a more compassionate and hopeful account of Hagar's and Ishmael's experiences in the wilderness. Post-expulsion, Abraham did not abandon them to their fate but rather made provisions for their journey. Ibn Abbas, the Prophet's uncle narrates that under divine inspiration, Abraham accompanied Hagar and Ishmael on their journey to Mecca's site. Abraham made them sit under the bush, placed a leather bag containing some dates and a small waterskin near them, and set out homeward. Hagar followed him, saying: "O Abraham! Why are you leaving us in this valley where there is no one we can enjoy the company of, nor is there anything else?" She repeated that to him many times, but he did not look back at her. Then she asked him: "Has God ordered you to do so?" He said: "Yes." She said: "Then He will not neglect us."

The Zamzam Spring

When the water ran out Hagar and Ishmael became thirsty and dehydrated. She stared at Ishmael, tossing in agony. She left him, for she could not endure looking at the dying child. Hagar frantically searched for water between the hillocks of As-Safa and al-Marwa. She saw an angel at the Zamzam site, digging the earth till water flowed from that place. The narrative suggests a theological underpinning where Hagar's invocation during her desperate search for water is met with divine intervention, illustrating her integral role in the establishment of Islamic traditions. The legendary Zamzam well emphasizes God's mercy and provision for Hagar and Ishmael during their plight. They are portrayed not merely as casualties of familial strife but as pivotal figures in the eventual emergence of major monotheistic traditions in Arabia.

Make This Land Secure

From here, the Quran picks up Abraham's saga and his dysfunctional family. On his return journey, when Abraham was far enough away that Hagar could not see him, he raised both hands and invoked Allah. He said the following prayers according to the Quran: *"O my Sustainer! Make this land secure and grant its people fruitful sustenance - such as those who believe in Allah and the Last Day."* (2:126) "Grant its people fruitful sustenance," is the answer to one of the largest oil reserves in Saudi Arabia. According to the Bible, Abraham never contacted Ishmael or Hagar after abandoning them. However, Abraham often visited his family in Mecca in the Arabian account.

The Expulsion's Significance

The expulsion acts as a watershed moment, creating a genealogical and cultural schism between two significant lineages—the Israelites through Isaac and the Ishmaelites through Ishmael. The narrative showcases how themes of survival, faith, and divine mercy reshaped the discourse surrounding Hagar and Ishmael from one of mere victimhood to one of heritage and spirituality.

Contemporary Implications

The story of Hagar and Ishmael, set against the backdrop of their expulsion, reverberates strongly in the modern discourse surrounding Jewish-Arab relations. It reflects the broader tensions that persist in contemporary society today. In considering these complex cultural legacies, it becomes evident that the stories of Hagar and Ishmael encapsulate more than a familial conflict; they illustrate the enduring struggles for dignity, recognition, and belonging that resonate within the human experience today.

The Origin of the City of Mecca

Hagar settled near the Zamzam Well, which still flows today. It may have been that spring that induced a wandering group of Bedouin families belonging to the South Arabian (Qahtani) tribe of Jurhum to settle there. Ishmael married a girl of this tribe and became the progenitor of the Arabianized tribes. (In the Biblical account, Ishmael married a girl from Egypt since Hagar was also from there.) Thus, their descent was from a Hebrew father and a Qahtani mother.

Role of Ishmael in Building the Kabah

According to Ibn Abbas: "When Abraham thought of visiting his family he left in Mecca, and he told his wife (Sarah) of his decision. He found Ishmael behind the Zamzam well, mending his arrows. He said: 'O Ishmael, your Lord has ordered me to build a house for Him.' Ishmael said: 'Obey the order of your Lord.' Abraham replied: 'Allah has also ordered me that you should help me therein.' Ishmael replied: 'Then I will do so.'" When the building became too high for Abraham to lift more stones, he stood upon the stone of Al Maqam (station of Abraham) and kept handing Ishmael the rocks.

Ishmael in the Bible and Quran

The figure of Ishmael holds significant importance in Abrahamic religions, particularly in Judaism, Christianity, and Islam. While both the Bible and the Quran offer narratives about Ishmael, they present markedly different portrayals of him, which reflect complex theological implications for followers of these faith traditions.

Portrayal in the Bible

In the biblical narrative, Ishmael is depicted as the son of Abraham and Hagar, a slave woman. His birth follows a decision made by Abraham and his wife Sarah when they could not conceive a child naturally. Sarah's suggestion for Abraham to take Hagar as a wife underscores human effort to fulfill divine promises. (Genesis 16). The Bible conveys a stark sentiment regarding Ishmael's place within Abraham's lineage, often portraying him in an unfavorable light; for instance, he is characterized as a "wild donkey" in Genesis 16:12, indicating his allegedly rebellious and aggressive nature.

Ishmael is seen as the secondary son, overshadowed by Isaac's birthright, who is favored as the child of promise (Genesis 21:12-13). Furthermore, Ishmael's expulsion from the household alongside Hagar, at Sarah's behest, highlights themes of rejection and alienation. In the biblical context, this narrative establishes a clear distinction between the descendants of Isaac, who are viewed as the chosen people. In contrast, Ishmael's lineage is often relegated to a lesser status. This foundational narrative contributes to historical tensions and rivalries between Jews and Arabs, with Ishmaelite descendants identified with the latter.

Portrayal in the Quran

Conversely, the portrayal of Ishmael in the Quran presents a significantly different perspective. Within the Islamic tradition,

Ishmael, or Ismail, is honored as a prophet. He is recognized as a key figure in the establishment of a lineage that led to Prophet Muhammad, the final prophet of Islam. The Quran does not focus on inheritance and rivalries in the same way as the Bible; instead, it emphasizes Ishmael's dedication and obedience in the face of divine command. This adherence is particularly highlighted in the narrative surrounding Ishmael's near sacrifice, where he actively expresses faith and submission to Allah's will (Quran 37:102).

The Quranic portrayal of Ishmael carries significant implications. Firstly, it positions Ishmael as a figure of faith, compassion, and righteousness. He stands alongside his father as a model of God's obedience. This portrayal not only elevates his dignity but also fosters unity among the Islamic community regarding their heritage, as both Ishmael and Isaac are revered but do not denote supremacy over one another. Furthermore, Ishmael's narrative is tied closely to Islam's cultural and religious practices, such as the pilgrimage to Mecca (Hajj), which commemorates the legacy of Hagar and Ishmael (Quran 2:158).

Inter-religious Relationships and Theological Implications

In the biblical narrative, the negative connotations associated with Ishmael have historically contributed to tensions between Jewish and Arab identity, framing Ishmael's descendants as inferior outsiders. This portrayal underlines a historical context of conflict, exclusion, and division, which has persisted for centuries.

By contrast, the Quran encourages a vision of shared identity and piety that transcends ethnic boundaries. It portrays Ishmael as the forefather of many significant figures in Islamic history. It also shares reverence for Isaac's lineages. This emphasis on unity promotes inter-religious dialogue and a more inclusive understanding of the Abrahamic covenant.

The Quran also reflects a broader theological and moral stance that upholds mercy, compassion, and divine justice. By recognizing both brothers and their respective lineages without prioritizing one over the other, the Islamic tradition fosters diverse paths of faith. These paths hold the potential for reconciliation in contemporary contexts marked by interfaith tension.

IDEOLOGICAL CONFLICT BETWEEN PROPHET MUHAMMAD AND THE JEWS

CHAPTER 6

PROPHET MUHAMMAD CONTACT WITH THE JEWS

This chapter explores the interactions between Prophet Muhammad and the Jewish tribes in Medina. Initially, these interactions were marked by mutual respect and cooperation. However, as theological and political differences emerged, tensions grew, leading to conflicts. The chapter delves into the ideological conflicts between Prophet Muhammad and the Jews, examining the historical context and consequences of these interactions.

Israelites' Struggle is Inspiration for Muslims

Prophet Muhammad, a direct descendant of Prophet Ishmael, received divine revelation around 610. This was during a period when he faced persecution from a pagan Meccan society that thrived on idolatry and moral corruption. Prophet Muhammad and a small number of his followers were persecuted for their beliefs. Mecca had no Jewish or Christian communities. Yet the story of Moses is told in the Quran in significant detail during the Mecca period. It is because the Arabs were familiar with the story of Moses. Secondly. Muslims in Mecca were suppressed and disinherited, struggling in an unbelieving society. They were persecuted for their exclusive monotheistic beliefs. Their plight was comparable to that of the Israelites before them (28:4-5), and how a small band of believers under the leadership of legendary warrior prophet Moses overcame Pharaoh, the mighty man alive at that time. The Quran's allusions to the Israelites' deliverance reaffirmed the notion that a small, faith-based community could triumph over a dominant, oppressive force. This theme of resilience and divine support would inspire the early Muslims as they confronted their adversities in the face of exclusion.

Contact with Jews: A Complex Relationship

The relationship between Prophet Muhammad and the Jewish tribes in Medina is a significant historical narrative characterized by initial hope, mutual respect, and ultimately escalating into conflicts. This complex interaction offers insights into the early Islamic community's struggles that resonate throughout religious history. The journey from admiration to contention between Muslims and Jews reflects not only the socio-political realities of the time but also the theological underpinnings of the faith that shape their identities. Initially, the conflict was limited to ideological warfare and later resulted in armed confrontation. This chapter deals with ideological warfare between Jews and Muslims in Medina.

The Jews of Medina

In 622, the Prophet and a small band of believers who were persecuted for 12 years in Mecca, migrated to Medina - an oasis town about two hundred miles north of Mecca. A story very similar to the migration of Abraham from Iraq to Palestine. The Prophet arrived in Medina to arbitrate a bloody civil war between the two Arab tribes, the Khazraj and the Aws. Jewish clans, and their clients, were embroiled in conflict on opposite sides. Medina's Jews were divided and killed each other while fighting for the pagan Arabs. Judaism was well-established in Medina two centuries before the Prophet Muhammad's birth. Some records indicate more than twenty Jewish clans, including three prominent ones: the Banu **Nadir**, the Banu **Qaynuqa**, and the Banu **Qurayza**. Although influential, Jews did not rule the oasis. Instead, they were clients of two large pagan Arab tribes, the Khazraj and the Aws, who protected them in return for feudal loyalty.

Various traditions uphold different views, and it is unclear whether Medina's Jewish clans were Arabized Jews or Arabs who practiced Jewish monotheism. Indeed, they were Arabic speakers with Arab names. One possibility is that their ancestors settled in Hijaz when they were expelled from Palestine at various times.

The Prophet's Friendly Overtures

Fasting: The Prophet bound himself to the Jews in friendship and respect because they were monotheists. He supported the Jews so fervently that he fasted with them. During the early Medina period, Ramadan fasting was not yet instituted. (It was 624 CE when the first Ramadan was observed in Medina.) Since the Jews were the people of the first scripture, it was logical to follow their example.

Direction of Prayer: The Prophet prayed facing Jerusalem as the Jews did. Even during the Mecca period, whenever the Prophet offered prayers in the Kabah, he faced northward to both the Kabah and Jerusalem. When he moved to Medina, he continued to pray northward toward Jerusalem.

Medina constitution: The Prophet incorporated religious freedom, which became human history's first charter of conscience freedom. The Medina Constitution guaranteed complete freedom of religion and **equality** for Jews. "The Jews who attach themselves to our commonwealth shall be protected from all insults and vexations. They shall have equal rights to assistance and good offices among our people. The Jews of various branches and all others domiciled in Yathrib (Medina) shall form with the Muslims **one composite nation.** They shall **practice their religion as freely as the Muslims** and the clients and allies of the Jews shall enjoy the same security and freedom." There was, however, no express stipulation that Jews should formally recognize Muhammad as the Messenger and Prophet of God. No tax was levied upon the Jews because they were expected to defend Medina. Many Jews welcomed the civil war ended in the oasis. With the reconciliation between the two Arab tribes and the addition of the third, the Jewish community, the dawn of peace in the oasis seemed imminent.

Bias of Western Historian

Several Western historians misconstrued the Prophet's friendly gestures. They opined that when the Apostle left Mecca, he looked forward to his acceptance by the Jews of Yathrib. He tried to win them over by adopting Jewish practices. However, the Apostle was soon disappointed by Jewish rejection, so he broke up with them and crushed them. This picture represents a contorted reflection of events. In two early Meccan surahs (10:93 and 17:4-5), the Prophet warned about Jews' contentiousness. Despite this warning, he extended friendship to the Jewish community based on the principle of presumption of innocence. The Jews were fellow monotheists.

Expectations of the Jewish Community

There is no evidence that the Apostle ever considered Medina's Jews converting to Islam. Since Jews worshipped One God and their religion was given equal status to Islam, there was no expectation nor incentive to become Muslims. Like Christianity, Islam is an evangelizing religion, seeking new converts to the faith. It was not surprising that Medina Jews were invited to Islam by the Prophet and his companions. However, Jews remained faithful to their faith, with some exceptions. Medina's Muslims, at the least, expected understanding from their fellow monotheists in their struggle with Mecca. However, the euphoria did not last long and was replaced by harsh political realities. Relations with several Jewish tribes in Medina became tense. It was still a precarious situation for Muslims and the Prophet Muhammad in Medina in these early months.

The Jewish Opposition

Moreover, the Quran addressed this ideological clash, often reiterating the notion that Jews had deviated from the true essence of their own scriptures. Although this critical tone has led to accusations of anti-Jewish sentiment within the Quran, it is crucial to note that the text reserves its most severe criticisms for the idol-worshipping Arabs of Prophet Muhammad's time. Thus, accusations made against the Jews of Medina must be understood within the Quran's broader context of advocating for a unified monotheistic belief system. This transcends specific ethnic or religious identities.

Religious Reasons

Out of their selfish envy, many among the followers of earlier revelation would like to bring you back to denying the truth after you have attained faith - [even] after the truth has become clear to them. Nonetheless, forgive and forbear until God manifests His will: behold, God has the power to will anything. (2:109)

The Jews regarded their religion as a national heritage reserved for the children of Israel alone. They did not believe in the necessity or possibility of an additional revelation. As the "chosen people," prophets rose from their tribes. Muhammad's prophethood was incompatible with their understanding of Judaism.

Increased Political Clout

The Prophet's teachings and leadership profoundly affected the people who joined Islam, and their conversion consolidated and increased Muslim power in Medina. The Prophet became the most powerful man in Medina as Islam spread throughout the clans of Aws and Khazraj. His power seemed likely to increase.

Regaining Political Supremacy

Medina's Jews hoped to recover political supremacy; a hope extinguished by Prophet Muhammad's successes. The union of the two dominant tribes of Al Aws and Al Khazraj, and with the addition of Muslim immigrants to the new ummah, the Jews felt disenfranchised. They saw their political position in Medina decline. At this stage, the Jews began to rethink their position vis-à-vis Muhammad. They asked themselves whether they should let his call, spiritual power, and authority spread while remaining satisfied with the security they enjoyed under his protection and the increased trade and wealth that his peace had brought to their city.

Jewish Ideological Assault

The Jews used their Old Testament knowledge to criticize Prophet Muhammad's claim that the Quran was God's speech. For Muhammad, the idea that he was a prophet receiving messages from God and with a commission from Him was the basis of the whole political and religious movement he led. Remove this idea, and the movement collapses. The intellectual conflict between Prophet Muhammad and the Jews became very bitter as it threatened Islam's core. Once they rejected Prophet Muhammad, the Jews had to justify this decision, at least to themselves. Perhaps this was why they mocked Prophet Muhammad.

Active Hostilities by the Jews

Having disagreements on religious matters, the Jews became hostile to the Prophet. There was verbal abuse of the Prophet, his wives, and the Muslim community. Despite various peace treaties with the Prophet, Jews actively supported Muhammad's enemies, the Pagans of Mecca. They did everything to destroy Islam and Muslims.

Potential For Destruction of The Muslim Community

Muslims and Prophet Muhammad's position in Medina was still precarious. If many Muslims thought what the Jews said was true, the community's whole structure would unravel. The Prophet needed men who believed deeply in his religious mission. The Jews tried to remove his support.

Therefore, the vigorous Quranic defense of Islam was the need of the hour to counterbalance the anti-Islamic accusations of Medinese Jews, potentially threatening the Muslim community's existence. With this background information, the Quranic criticism of Jews must be understood. Although the Quran is critical of Jews for deviating from their revealed scripture, it reserved its harsh condemnation for Arab contemporaries of the Prophet. They worshipped idols and rejected monotheism.

The criticism of Jews in the Quran is a lesson for Muslims as to how to avoid the errors of Jews. By following the Quran's method, the story of the Children of Israel is an object lesson for all believers in God of whatever community or time. It highlights how the Quran addresses various accusations and misconceptions propagated by Jewish communities during Prophet Muhammad's time. The chapter delves into specific verses answering Jewish criticism that challenged the legitimacy of Muhammad's prophethood and the authenticity of the Quran.

Conclusion

The interactions between Prophet Muhammad and the Jewish tribes of Medina encapsulate the profound complexities of religious identity, community cohesion, and ideological divergence. While the initial relationship was characterized by mutual respect and cooperative governance, shifting political dynamics, coupled with ideological disputes, ultimately led to conflict and estrangement. Understanding this relationship is essential for Muslims, as it sheds light on the mechanisms of interfaith dialogue and the perils of animosity based on misunderstanding. The legacy of this early encounter remains relevant in contemporary discussions about coexistence and respect among diverse faith traditions. It urges believers to learn from the past in pursuit of a harmonious future.

CHAPTER 7

ISLAM: A CONTINUATION OF ABRAHAM'S MONOTHEISM

"Islam is a false religion" was a common criticism of the Jews of Medina. It was perhaps due to misunderstanding and lack of knowledge about its historical and theological foundations. In response to this charge, the Quran meets this intellectual challenge by stressing that Islam is not a new religion, and it represents the true continuation of Abraham's pristine monotheism. This chapter emphasizes pure worship of one God and a return to Abraham's original teachings. Islam maintains the essence of Abraham's monotheism and highlights the shared heritage among Jews, Christians, and Muslims. Thus, the argument stands that rather than questioning Islam's validity, one should recognize it as a restoration of Abraham's original monotheism.

Abraham's Faith and Monotheism

The Quran highlights the guiding principles of the Abrahamic faith. It presents itself not as a new religion, but as the rightful successor to Abraham's monotheism. Quran 6:161 articulates a declaration that *"Say: "My Sustainer has guided me along the straight path through the ever-true faith. The way of Abraham, who turned away from all that is false, and was not of those who ascribe divinity to aught beside Him." (6:161)* This fundamental premise underscores that any claim to possessing the true path lies with those who follow Abraham's way of life, as reiterated in Quran 3:68: *"The people with the right to claim Abraham are surely those who follow him—as does this Prophet and all who believe [in him]—and God is near the believers."* This message is critical because it establishes a continuum from Abraham to Muhammad. It also identifies the latter as a prophet of the same faith lineage.

The Primacy of Abraham

O followers of earlier revelations! Why do you argue about Abraham, seeing that the Torah and the Gospel were not revealed until long after him? Will you not, then, use your reason? (3:65) And they say, "Be Jews"—or "Be Christians"—"and you shall be on the right path." Say: "No, but [ours is] the creed of Abraham, who shunned away from all that is false, and was not of those who ascribe divinity to anything besides God." (2:135)

Abraham's identity is pivotal in understanding the relationship between Judaism, Christianity, and Islam. The Quran emphasizes that Abraham was neither a Jew nor a Christian; rather, he was a Muslim, in the Quranic terminology, has a much broader meaning: one who submits to God's will (Quran 3:67). Today, the term Muslim is misunderstood as the follower of Prophet Muhammad. These verses highlight a significant point: religious labels that arose after Abraham's time do not define his faith. The assertion that Islam is a restoration of Abraham's creed provides a solid foundation for Muslims to affirm their faith as aligned with the earliest forms of worship.

The Walking Path of Monotheism

Moreover, the Quran makes a compelling case against faith fragmentation into various denominations after Abraham. It critiques Jews and Christians' claims that exclusivity in faith pertains only to their respective religions. *"Say: 'No, but [ours is] the creed of Abraham, who shunned away from all that is false.'"* This insistence on a shared lineage reinforces the unity of purpose across all three Abrahamic faiths, suggesting that the distinctions between them are primarily human interpretations rather than divine commandments.

Abraham as the Father of the Faithful

Abraham is recognized not merely as a distant patriarch but as a principal figure whose legacy informs Islamic theology. In Quran 3:84, it confirms belief in *"what has been bestowed upon Abraham and Ishmael and Isaac and Jacob and their descendants."* This illustrates that while distinctions may emerge throughout religious history, the essence remains rooted in belief in one God.

Continuity of Divine Revelation

Say: "We believe in God, and in that which has been bestowed from on high upon us, and that which has been bestowed upon Abraham and Ishmael and Isaac and Jacob and their descendants, and that which has been vouchsafed by their Sustainer unto Moses and Jesus and all the [other] prophets: we make no distinction between any of them. And unto Him do we
surrender ourselves." (3:84)

To view Islam as a mere offshoot of earlier religious teachings is to overlook the Quran's foundational assertion that it is part of an unbroken chain of divine guidance. Islam claims to recognize and honor all previous prophets, as Quran 3:84 illustrates: *"We make no distinction between any of them."* This acknowledgment encourages an interfaith approach, allowing for dialogue across religious boundaries while asserting the continuity of faith originating from the same God.

The One God of All Prophets

And do not argue with the followers of earlier revelation otherwise than in a most kindly manner - unless it be such of them as are bent on evildoing - and say: "We believe in what has been bestowed from on high upon us, and what has been bestowed upon you. For our God and your God is one and the same, and it is unto Him that We [all] surrender ourselves." Thus, we have bestowed this divine writ from on high upon you [O Muhammad]. And they to whom we have vouchsafed this divine writ believe in it—just as among those [followers of earlier revelations] some believe in it. (29:46-47)

In the context of monotheistic traditions, it is imperative to approach the commonalities rather than the divergences. The Quran invites consideration through 29:46-47, encouraging its followers to recognize that followers of previous revelations worship the same God. The acknowledgment that one God sustains all sentient beings underlines the call for unity among believers. This shared theological ground calls for peaceful coexistence among the Abrahamic faiths.

Conclusion

In conclusion, Islam's claim to legitimacy is inherently linked to its portrayal as the continuation of Abraham's monotheism, which predates the distinctions of Judaism and Christianity. Rather than viewing Islam as a false religion, it is essential to recognize its role as the rightful heir to a tradition of pure, unaltered monotheism as practiced by its forefather, Abraham. By understanding Islam in this manner, adherents can appreciate their identity as part of a broader tradition that champions the worship of one, undivided God. This reflects the ultimate truth echoed through the ages by all prophets, including Moses, Jesus, and Muhammad.

CHAPTER 8

GOD'S CHOSEN PEOPLE

The Quran counters the virulent Islamophobic Jewish propaganda, gives a balanced view of Jewish history, and highlights the positive and negative aspects of their practices. The notion of Jews as "God's chosen people" is deeply rooted in Judaism's religious and cultural narrative, implying a special status and relationship with God. However, this idea has not reached unanimous acceptance, and it raises significant theological and historical debates. The Quran critically examines this idea, emphasizing the spiritual essence of chosenness rather than inherited privilege.

The Spiritual Basis of the "Chosen People"

The Jewish claim to being the chosen people is deeply embedded in the scriptures, prominently articulated in passages like Deuteronomy 7:6, which proclaims that *"you are a people consecrated to the LORD your God: of all the peoples on earth, the LORD your God chose you to be His treasured people."* As the only community professing monotheism at their time, they established a foundational paradigm that underscores a special divine relationship, reinforced by prophetic declarations such as God's promise in Isaiah 41:10 to uphold and strengthen His people.

From the Islamic perspective, while acknowledging the spiritual status of the Jews as previously chosen people, the Quran emphasizes this elevation as a phase in a broader divine plan. It recognizes the children of Israel as having received favor due to their previous adherence to monotheism. The Quran asserts, *"O Children of Israel! Remember the blessings of Mine with which I graced you and how I favored you above all other people." (2:47)* Thus, the Quran validates the historical significance of

Jews while framing it as part of a continuum that culminates in the final revelation to Prophet Muhammad.

Conditional Understanding of "Chosenness"

The concept of chosenness within Judaism conveys a covenantal relationship founded on moral and ethical obligations toward God, which is articulated in Exodus 19:5: *"Now if you will obey Me faithfully and keep My covenant, you shall be My treasured possession among all the peoples."* This conditional understanding is mirrored in the Quranic discourse, where it is made clear that God's covenant does not extend unconditionally to all descendants of Abraham. In verse 2:124, God states to Abraham, *"I shall make you a leader of men,"* followed by the stipulation that *"My covenant does not embrace evildoers."* This establishes that being chosen is contingent upon righteousness and loyalty to God's commandments.

The Quranic Rebuttal to Racially Based Chosenness

By contrast, the Quran critiques the idea that racially inherited status guarantees salvation or divine favor. Verses in the Quran indicate that members of Israel have deviated from the true message of Abraham, emphasizing that one's relationship with God is based on individual conduct rather than ancestral claims.

The Quran firmly rejects the idea of hereditary chosenness, countering racially or nationally based claims of superiority. The assertion of being God's chosen people must not perpetuate an exclusivist ideology; as seen in verse 4:49, *"Nay, but it is God who causes whomever He wills to grow in purity; and none shall be wronged by as much as a hair's breadth."* Here, the Quran addresses any potential supremacist ideology implied by Jewish claims, emphasizing that all humans, regardless of lineage, are equally accountable for their moral conduct and spiritual choices.

The Way of Righteousness

This sense of accountability is reiterated in Quran 2:83, where God commands the children of Israel to worship Him, uphold justice to their kinsfolk, be kind, and engage in prayer and charity. *"You shall worship none but God; and you shall do good unto your parents and kinsfolk, and the orphans, and the poor; and you shall speak unto all people in a kindly way; and you shall be constant in prayer; and you shall spend in charity." And yet, save for a few of you, you turned away: for you are obstinate folk!"* This is vital because, while the Old Testament also alludes to Israel's waywardness, as captured in passages outlining their rebellions and disobedience, the Quran emphasizes that righteousness, not lineage, determines one's standing before God.

Abandon the False Idea of "Chosen People"

Be not foremost among those who deny its truth; and do not barter away My messages for a trifling gain; and of Me, of Me be conscious! (2:41) The "trifling gain" is their conviction that they are "God's chosen people" and, by implication, superior to Gentiles - a claim that the Quran consistently refutes. This refers to the persistent Jewish belief that they, alone among all nations, have been graced by divine revelation.

Renew Your Bond with God and Man

Overshadowed by ignominy are they wherever they may be, save [when they bind themselves again] in a bond with God and men. (3:112) Anyone who commits evil will be punished accordingly. He will not find any protectors or patrons besides God. (4:123)

Thus, the Quran warns those who espouse supremacist ideologies to abandon their evil ways and renew their bonds with God. It also urges them to join the human family as equals. They will not be overshadowed by ignominy if they return to the concept of God as the Lord and Sustainer of all mankind. They should also give up the idea of being "Chosen people" (in a hereditary sense). They will be forgiven through God's mercy and grace otherwise they will be overshadowed by ignominy on Judgment Day.

Islamic Teachings

Islam rejects perceived superiority passed on by birth or circumstance rather than merit or work. Racist ideology is completely alien to Islam. No one enjoys special status. God's blessings are given to people based on merit, not group or race. Racism is a narcissistic phenomenon in degenerated societies. Any ideology that divides humanity into superior and inferior categories is inherently evil. That is what Pharaoh and Hitler did to the children of Israel. It contradicts the basic Islamic doctrine that all human beings are equal and only a man's character determines his status in God's sight.

The Prophet Said:

"Humanity came from Adam and Eve. Arabs have no superiority over a non-Arab, nor does a non-Arab have any superiority over an Arab; also, a white has no superiority over a black, nor has a black any superiority over a white except through piety and righteous actions."

Conclusion

The Quran presents a nuanced approach to chosenness by intertwining spiritual responsibility with moral accountability. It recontextualizes inherited identities, emphasizing righteousness and the shared legacy of monotheism rather than asserting racial superiority. By framing the discussion in terms of ethical living and communal responsibility, the Quran critiques supremacist ideologies. It advocates for the rights of all descendants of Abraham, compatible with the new divine revelations entrusted to Muhammad.

CHAPTER 9

THE QURAN'S CRITIQUE OF JEWISH NON-COMPLIANCE

WITH DIVINE COMMANDS

This chapter examines the Quranic perspective on Jewish non-compliance with divine commands. It highlights various instances where the Quran criticizes Jewish communities for their disobedience and failure to uphold the God covenant. It addresses issues such as the breaking of the Sabbath, the worship of the golden calf, and the rejection of prophets. It emphasizes the call for divine guidance and the consequences of straying from righteousness. The chapter also explores the broader implications of these critiques for interfaith relations and shared moral responsibilities among Abrahamic faiths. This scrutiny is not a blanket condemnation of all Jews but directed at specific groups and their inconsistencies. By citing both positive and negative aspects of Jewish religious history, the Quran furthers its argument. It is within this context that the Quran describes Jews' errors and answers their objections.

Non-Compliance with the Covenants

In Medina, the Jews upheld significant elements of the Torah. However, there is scholarly debate regarding their depth of understanding of the Talmud and Jewish scholarship. These tribes engaged in internal conflicts, choosing sides with opposing Arab factions (the Aws and Khazraj), which resulted in fratricide and the violation of their sacred obligation not to harm one another. The Quran explicitly condemns this hypocrisy, stating: *"And Lo! We accepted your solemn pledge that you would not shed one another's blood and drive one another out of your homeland... And yet, it is you who slay one another and expel some of your people." (2:84-8)* This inconsistency serves as a broader critique of their spiritual state, highlighting a relationship with God that was superficial and unreflective of true devotion.

The Ezra Controversy

The Jewish assertion that Ezra is God's son emerges as a focal point of discord. The Quran critiques this claim, implying that such beliefs lead to divine misrepresentation. The phrase "son of God" possesses disparate meanings in Jewish and Christian theology. Judaism suggests a divinely favored individual rather than divine kinship. For instance, Jewish people are often called "children of God" due to their covenantal relationship with Him. In Christianity, the term is uniquely and literally associated with Jesus Christ as God's incarnate son. This theological divergence is pivotal, as the Quran's criticism is directed not at Judaism in its entirety, but at specific beliefs held by certain factions within that community.

Moreover, historical accounts reveal that many Jews acknowledged Ezra's significant contributions to Jewish law and identity but rejected any divine status. Arabian Jews' viewpoint - equating Ezra with a divine figure — was not representative of wider Jewish thought. This inconsistency is emblematic of the broader tensions evident in Medina where fragmented allegiances often compromised shared religious values.

Uncharitable Disposition and Materialism

The Quran also critiques Jews' disposition toward material wealth, suggesting a misguided prioritization of worldly gain over spiritual accountability. For example, the text asserts: *"But those who miserly cling to all that God has granted them out of His bounty — this is a curse for them." (3:180)* This notion that material possessions can somehow confer a privileged status is fundamentally challenged, emphasizing that divine favor and wealth are not inherently linked. The critique addresses a pervasive materialism that obscures spiritual responsibilities, ultimately suggesting that such attachments contribute to their moral decline.

Breaking the Sabbath in Pursuit of Gain

The Quran further denounces certain Jews who disregarded the Sabbath, a fundamental law and sign of their covenant with God. The narrative recounts their attempts to trap fish — an act explicitly prohibited on the Sabbath — which led to divine retribution, symbolically described as being transformed into apes. This allegorical expression emphasizes the severity of their actions, utilizing vivid imagery to illustrate how easily one can forsake divine commands for transient gains. The fundamental inconsistency of disregarding the Sabbath while profiting from its prohibition highlights a moral failing. This is deeply at odds with the Torah's values.

Failure to Propagate Monotheism

Central to the Quran's critique is Jews' failure to uphold their role as a "light unto the nations." The text emphasizes that they were entrusted with the Torah not solely for personal edification but as a guide for all humanity. However, the deeply entrenched view of Judaism as a solely ethnocentric faith has often led to a reluctance to share its profound monotheistic insights with others. This results in an insular approach that stands in stark contrast to Islam's universal message.

Light Unto the Nations

"I the LORD have called unto you in righteousness, and have taken hold of your hand, and submitted you as the people's covenant, as a light unto the nations" (Isaiah 42:6).

Many Jews today are secular Jews. Evidently, they rejected the Torah, so their "light unto nations" is irrelevant. Are modern-day Israeli Jews "light onto nations?" Sadly, the answer is no. Instead of bringing light, they caused death, destruction, and darkness. The puzzling question is how Jews of all peoples, who have been persecuted for thousands of years, now collaborate with the same racist and antisemitic persecutors. Amnesty International has analyzed Israel's intent to create and maintain a system of oppression and dominance over Palestinians. It has examined its key components: territorial fragmentation; segregation and control; land and property dispossession; and the denial of economic and social rights. It has concluded that this system amounts to apartheid.

Conclusion

The Quranic criticisms of Medina's Jewish community highlight significant theological and ethical positions, emphasizing a discrepancy between beliefs and practices that embody a broader moral failing. The texts compel reflection on the nature of religious obligations, the relationship between societal behavior and spiritual truth, and the imperative to uphold a universal message of monotheism. These critiques illuminate the dynamics of faith, accountability, and community, urging a return to the core tenets of divine expectation and moral responsibility.

The Consequences of Breaking the Covenant

Forbidden Foods

Judaism's dietary laws, called Kashrut, are fundamental to Jewish identity, spirituality, and cultural heritage. These laws encompass a variety of prohibitions, including certain foods deemed "impure" or unclean. The Quran asserts that specific dietary restrictions imposed on Jews were a punishment for their transgressions as illustrated in various verses.

Historical Context of Dietary Restrictions

Jewish tradition says dietary laws stem from the Mosaic law in the Torah. These laws reflect God's commandments that govern which foods are permissible and which are prohibited. This is articulated in Leviticus 11, which details kosher animals and non-kosher animals. The implications are clear: these restrictions serve not only as guidelines for spiritual living but also as symbols of a broken covenant between God and the Jewish people. The Quran states that *"to those who followed the Jewish faith did We forbid all beasts with claws," (6:146)* which emphasizes that these restrictions were uniquely placed upon the Jewish people as retribution for their prior misdeeds.

The Role of Obedience and Disobedience

According to the Quran, the severe dietary laws imposed on the Jews were a direct consequence of their previous disobedience. As articulated in Surah Al-Baqarah, *"For the wickedness committed by those who followed the Jewish faith, We denied them certain good things of life which were allowed to them." (4:160)* The refrain of disobedience resonates throughout the Quran, reiterating that this punishment was not arbitrary but rather a means to remind the Children of Israel of their covenant with God. The concept of dietary laws as a test of obedience is significant for both Jews and Muslims. This suggests that adherence to these rules facilitates spiritual growth and promotes individual accountability before God.

The Scattering of the Jewish People

The term "wandering Jews of the diaspora" refers to the scattering of Jewish communities throughout the world because of their disobedience. This dispersion is seen as divine punishment. It not only physically separates the Jewish people but also diminishes communal and cultural coherence. The sustained existence of these laws, even in diverse circumstances, fuels Jewish identity and offers continuity amid historical challenges.

WAR BETWEEN PROPHET MUHAMMAD AND THE JEWS

CHAPTER 10

THE EXPULSION OF BANU QAYNUQA: FACT OR FICTION?

The expulsion of the Jewish tribe Banu Qaynuqa from Medina is a historical event shrouded in uncertainty, speculation, and controversy. The narrative surrounding this episode is predominantly derived from early Islamic historians, notably Ibn Ishaq. His accounts are marred by reliability questions due to the absence of a credible transmission chain and significant temporal gaps. As noted by scholars such as Malik ibn Anas and Ibn Hajar, the stories involving Prophet Muhammad and the Jewish tribes of Medina have been criticized for being based on biased accounts, particularly from the sons of Jewish and pagan Arab converts. This skepticism invites a careful examination of the historical context, motivations, and discrepancies that characterize the account of Banu Qaynuqa's expulsion. This will challenge its veracity.

The Aftermath of the Battle of Badr

In the wake of the Battle of Badr, where Prophet Muhammad's followers achieved a surprising victory against the Meccan Quraysh, the political landscape in Medina became increasingly complex. The success of the nascent Muslim community was perceived as a direct threat to the political aspirations of the Jewish tribes in the region, notably Banu Qaynuqa. Tensions existed as the Jewish tribes sought to maintain their influence. This led to an atmosphere charged with anti-Islamic sentiments from certain Jewish poets and factions, which heightened the conflict leading to the expulsion narrative.

The Incident that Sparked Conflict

The traditional account maintains that friction erupted in the Qaynuqa marketplace following an altercation involving a Muslim woman and a Jewish goldsmith. The incident escalated, resulting in a Muslim killing the goldsmith, followed by brutal retaliation from the Jews. This further ignited hostility between the two groups. This antagonistic backdrop set the stage for Muhammad to confront the Banu Qaynuqa, warning them of impending divine retribution. The Jews reportedly challenged Muhammad, asserting their combat readiness, and rejecting any notion of weakness simply because of Muslim victories against the Quraysh.

The Siege of Banu Qaynuqa

Following their defiance, Prophet Muhammad besieged the Banu Qaynuqa for fifteen days. Abd Allah ibn Ubayy, a local leader with ties to the Qaynuqa, intervened during the siege, insisting on mercy for his allies. This intervention led Prophet Muhammad to reconsider his course of action. Instead of executing the Banu Qaynuqa, he expelled them from Medina.

Historical Inconsistencies

Several historical inconsistencies raise doubts about the traditional narrative surrounding Banu Qaynuqa's expulsion:

- The strongest argument against Banu Qaynuqa's expulsion is the lack of mention in the Quran. It documents the expulsion of al-Nadir and does not mention the alleged expulsion of B. Qaynuqa when both events were similar in importance. Surat al-Hashr deals with the banishment of the Jewish tribe, B. al-Nadir, from Medina and refers to their expulsion as "the **first** gathering."

- It is rather curious that the Qaynuqa, as dealers in arms and armor, could be trusted not to use them. They had more combat fighters than Muslims and they still surrendered?
- Notably, the account lacks meticulous detail regarding the alleged dishonor of the Arab woman, with some sources failing to mention it entirely.
- Yahya B. Adam reports that the B. al-Nadir were the first to be deported from Yathrib, not Qaynuqa.
- Imam Shafi mentions that the Apostle employed Jewish auxiliaries of B. Qaynuqa against the Jews of Khaybar.

Conclusion

The historical worthiness of the Banu Qaynuqa expulsion narrative is questionable due to numerous inconsistencies and an evident lack of robust documentation in primary Islamic texts and historical accounts. While it is essential to avoid outright dismissal of these sources, an analytical viewpoint reveals that the reality of events may be far more nuanced than the traditional accounts suggest. The preponderance of evidence favors a less dramatic resolution than collective expulsion. This hints at a potential targeted exile of key leaders within the tribe. This episode illustrates the delicate interplay of power, theology, and societal norms in the formative years of Islamic governance. This necessitates a careful review of the narratives that surround it.

CHAPTER 11

THE TREACHERY OF BANU AL-NADIR

AN EXAMINATION OF BETRAYAL AND ITS CONSEQUENCES

The historical narrative surrounding the Banu al-Nadir, a Jewish tribe in Medina, provides critical insights into the complexities of early Islamic society, particularly during the time of the Prophet Muhammad. Their violation of pacts and cooperation with hostile forces against Muslims not only led to their downfall but also highlighted the inherent risks of alliances based solely on self-interest and hypocrisy.

This chapter explores the treason committed by the Banu al-Nadir, focusing on their betrayal of pacts with the Muslim community, and the subsequent military action taken against them resulting in their expulsion from Medina. It is through understanding the past, particularly the betrayal by the Banu al-Nadir, that we can better appreciate the foundations upon which the early Muslim community was built and the lessons that continue to resonate today.

Violations of the Treaty

Shortly after his followers' exodus from Mecca to Medina, the Prophet concluded a treaty with the Banu al-Nadir of mutual non-interference and pledged neutrality in hostilities between Muslims and Quraysh.

- Within three months of the battle of Badr, the Nadir chief secretly entertained two hundred Meccan riders in their abortive attempt to attack Medina.
- In a year, the Meccans were ready to fight again. The Apostle had already been informed of al-Nadir's secret contacts with Mecca's Quraysh when they encamped at Uhud before the battle. They incited them to fight and informed them of Muslims' shortcomings.
- After the Muslims' setback at Uhud, the al-Nadir treacherously broke their contract with the Prophet Muhammad and allied with the Meccan Quraysh to destroy the Muslim community.

The Muslim Missionaries Massacre

Shortly after the Battle of Uhud, the Banu Amir approached Prophet Muhammad requesting Muslim missionaries to invite their people to Islam. Although apprehensive, the Prophet eventually complied after Abu Bara, a leader of the Banu Amir, promised safe passage for the missionaries. Tragically, at Bir Mauna, these emissaries were ambushed, resulting in their deaths except one. On his way home, he saw two men from B. Amir lying asleep. Not knowing that B. Amir had taken no direct part in the massacre, he killed both to avenge his companions.

The Assassination Plot Against the Prophet

Under a pact with B. al-Amir, the Apostle and the Jewish clan of B. al-Nadir were obliged to pay monetary compensation for the murder of two men. The Prophet visited Banu al-Nadir to discuss compensation obligations. During this visit, Huyayy ibn Akhtab, chief of Banu al-Nadir, conspired to assassinate the Prophet by suggesting that one of his tribesmen drop a stone on the Prophet from a roof. The plan was thwarted when the Prophet received divine revelation regarding the conspiracy, allowing him to escape unharmed. This incident marked a clear violation of their treaty with the Prophet. It demonstrated their willingness to betray even the sacred bonds of hospitality and safety established within the community. The crime of treason is defined as betraying one's country, especially by attempting to kill the sovereign or overthrow the government.

As tensions escalated, Prophet Muhammad sieged their fortifications in March 625. After a prolonged standoff lasting twenty-one days, where Muslims cut down palm trees to weaken enemy defenses, the Banu al-Nadir surrendered. They were given the option to leave Medina with all their movable possessions but not their arms, a decision they reluctantly accepted. This expulsion not only served as a punitive measure against their treachery but also reinforced the necessity for loyalty and integrity among Medina's diverse tribes.

Conclusion: The Aftermath and Prophetic Predictions

The actions of the Banu al-Nadir and their ultimate expulsion serve as compelling case studies of the consequences of betrayal within a community striving for cohesion and unity. The surah that reflects on this conflict, Al-Hashr, encapsulates the divine lessons learned from these events, underscoring the importance of loyalty to communal commitments. Their legacy reminds us of the vital bonds necessary for peaceful coexistence. As history demonstrated, those who failed to uphold these bonds ultimately faced collective punishment but also profound consequences in the afterlife. This is shown in Quranic verses foretelling divine retribution for their actions. This reflection encourages modern societies to evaluate their commitments to communal safety and integrity. This will foster deeper bonds that resist treachery's divisiveness.

CHAPTER 12

THE BANU QURAYZAH MASSACRE: FACT OR FICTION?

The incident of the massacre of Banu Qurayzah in early Islamic history serves as a pivotal moment. It has themes of betrayal, justice, and intercommunal relations in Medina. As historians and scholars grapple with the accuracy of accounts surrounding this event, significant questions arise regarding narratives presented in religious texts and historical documentation. This chapter explores the authenticity of the Banu Qurayzah massacre. It examines numerous aspects—including prerequisite alliances, betrayals, and the interpretation of relevant Quranic verses—that suggest that the traditional narrative may be embellished or lack substantial veracity.

Betrayal and Allegiance

The Banu Qurayzah tribe was initially allied with Prophet Muhammad and the Muslim community in Medina. However, as tensions escalated during the siege led by the Quraysh and their allies, the Qurayzah's allegiances shifted. Evidence within Islamic records accuses Banu Qurayzah of treachery, stating that they openly sided with the Meccan forces during the Battle of the Trench. This act of betrayal is commonly cited as the catalyst for their besiegement and subjugation. However, it remains crucial to scrutinize their involvement and motivations. Banu Qurayzah's apparent decision to act against Prophet Muhammad could stem from pragmatic concerns regarding their safety amidst the volatile circumstances they faced during the siege. Maybe Banu Qurayzah chose the winning party. The odds of Muslims surviving the battle of Trench were heavily against them. The Prophet besieged Banu Qurayzah's fort for twenty-five nights.

The Consultation Process

Following the Muslims' siege, the Banu Qurayzah sought mediation in the form of Abu Lubabah, requesting consultation before surrendering to Prophet Muhammad. Abu Lubabah confirmed their fate by indicating their probable execution—a sign that reflects deep apprehension among the tribe. However, the narrative leads to the selection of Saad ibn Muadh of the Banu Aws tribe, as an arbitrator. The Banu Qurayzah expected leniency based on prior relations, yet the verdict proclaimed by Saad culminated in severe punishment, including the execution of the men.

Historical-Critical Examination

The Quranic Basis for Rejecting the Story

- *And He brought down from their strongholds those followers of earlier revelation who had aided the aggressors and cast terror into their hearts. Some you slew, some you made captive, and He made you heirs to their lands, houses, and goods. (33:26-27)*

The Banu Qurayzah, anticipating the community's vengeance, which they had betrayed, withdrew to their fortresses near Medina. The Quran's reference to the story is extremely brief, and there is no indication of large-scale killing. Previously, the whole surah was devoted to explaining Banu Nadir's expulsion from Medina. One would think that if 600 or 900 people were killed in this manner, the event's significance would have been greater. There would have been a clear reference in the Quran, a conclusion drawn, and a lesson learned. But when only the guilty leaders were executed, it would be normal to expect only a brief reference. *"Some you slew" refers to the guilty leaders in the treason, and "Some you made captive" refers to the able-bodied adult fighters.*

Many historians reference Quranic verses as foundations for understanding the Banu Qurayzah massacre. The context and interpretation of these verses offer limited insights into the explicit and large-scale slaughter of Qurayzah men. The brevity of the verses and their lack of detailed accounts regarding mass executions support a broader perspective. This might imply punishing ringleaders rather than wholesale slaughter.

Logical Discrepancies in the Massacre Narrative

When critically examining the traditional accounts of the Banu Qurayzah incident, various logical inconsistencies emerge. If, as some reports suggest, hundreds were executed, it raises practical issues regarding logistics and the treatment of such a significant number of prisoners following their surrender.

- If 600-900 men and their families or roughly two to three thousand men, women, and children forced them to walk several hours to Medina. None of these prisoners tried to escape, and Muslims seem to have no difficulty locking up these tame prisoners.
- Surprisingly, a general of Muhammad's astute knowledge of strategy and logistics would have brought all these captives, making them walk many hours to Medina.
- They were all confined to the house of a woman named Bint al-Harith and bound with ropes. The question arises: how spacious was her house? If the prisoners were only the ring leaders, placing them in one house makes sense.
- Then to slay six to nine hundred fighting men and bury them in the middle of the town. It would have been far better, safer, and more efficient to execute them outside their forts. Take only women and children to Medina.

- Furthermore, witnesses and accounts noting a lack of visible remnants of such a massacre compound the skepticism surrounding this narrative.
- The following day, trenches were dug in the marketplace to bury the executed men. There was a ready-made trench dug outside Medina only a month ago, not far from the marketplace; why dig another trench, especially in the middle of town?
- Why were the Banu Qurayza targeted when the other Jewish groups who surrendered before or after them were treated leniently and allowed to leave?

How To Treat War Prisoners According to The Quran?

- *Had it not been for a decree from God that had already gone forth, there would indeed have been tremendous chastisement on account of all [the captives] that you took. (8:68)* This verse is a reference to the Battle of Badr where Muslims took many prisoners of war. According to some of the Prophet's companions, they should all be executed for their previous crimes against the Muslim community. Prisoners of war were routinely put to death in pre-Islamic Arabia. The "tremendous chastisement" that might have befallen the Muslims if they killed war prisoners. The killing of captives would have been a grave sin.
- [Hence], *O Prophet, say to the captives in your hands: "If God finds any good in your hearts, He will give you something better than all that has been taken from you and forgive you your sins, for God is much-forgiving, a dispenser of grace." And should they but seek to play false with you—well, they were false to God [Himself] before this, but He gave [the believers] mastery over them. And God is all-knowing and wise. (8:70-71)*
- *When you meet [at war], you overcome them fully and tighten their bonds. But after that [set them free] either by grace or against ransom, so that the burden of war may be lifted: thus [shall it be]. (47:4)*

The considerations surrounding the treatment of prisoners in earlier battles, particularly during the Battle of Badr, advocate humane treatment, preservation of life, and potential opportunities for redemption through Islam. Moreover, widespread punitive measures enacted against Banu Qurayzah appear inconsistent with the larger Islamic moral framework established in the Quran. This framework emphasizes justice while indicating that the burden of sin must not fall upon innocents.

Conclusion

Considering the evidence presented, the account of the massacre of Banu Qurayzah poses several critical questions regarding its authenticity and factual basis. Discrepancies in the historical narrative, the Quranic context, and the logical implications of warfare practices during the Prophet's time suggest that the common portrayal of the massacre may be significantly exaggerated or forged. It is essential to approach historical interpretations with a discerning eye, recognizing that the lens through which history is conveyed often reflects more than mere fact. Although Banu Qurayzah's events were rooted in historical facts, the overarching story that followed requires further examination. Thus, the emphasis should remain on the principles of justice articulated within Islamic teachings. These principles stand in contrast to the alleged scale of the Banu Qurayzah massacre depicted in existing lore.

CHAPTER 13

WAR AGAINST THE JEWS OF KHAYBAR

The Battle of Khaybar, fought in 628 CE, marks a pivotal moment in early Islamic history. It centers on the confrontation between the growing Muslim community and the Jewish tribes residing in the fertile oasis of Khaybar. This oasis is located approximately ninety miles north of Medina. This fortified territory served as a refuge for the exiled Jewish tribe of Banu Nadir. This tribe was heavily involved in efforts to undermine the nascent Muslim state, particularly during the Battle of the Trench.

Historical Context of Khaybar

Khaybar was characterized by its strong fortifications and strategic location, making it a crucial player in early Medina's power dynamics. Khaybar's historical backdrop illustrates the tension between Jewish tribes and the Muslim community. This tension is underscored by the exiled Banu Nadir's plot against the Prophet. Sallam ibn Abu al-Huqayq, Khaybar chieftain acted as the instigator of the Battle of Trench. He mobilized alliances with non-Muslim tribes, including the Banu Ghatafan, to destabilize the Prophet's authority in Medina.

The strategic significance of Khaybar was further emphasized by the sociopolitical landscape, where the threat of a coordinated attack from the Jewish tribes loomed large. Prophet Muhammad's wartime objectives were not merely punitive but aimed at securing peace and stability for the Muslim community, which had faced repeated betrayals and threats from the Jews of Medina and their allies.

Fighting is Prohibited for War Gains

As soon as you [O believers] are about to embark on a war that promises material gains, those who stayed behind [in the past] will surely say, "allow us to come with you"— [thus showing that] they would like to alter God's word. Say: "By no means shall you travel with us: God has declared aforetime [to whom all spoils of war shall belong]." Thereupon they will [surely] answer, "You begrudge us [our share of booty]!" They can grasp but so little of the truth! (48:15)

Quranic principles regarding warfare are paramount to understanding the motivations behind the Islamic war against Khaybar. The verse from Surah Al-Fath (48:15) contextualizes this confrontation by warning those who previously failed to support the cause of Islam while seeking material gains from warfare. This revelation called upon true believers, those who joined the Prophet during the Treaty of Hudaybiyyah, to engage solely based on their faith. This was rather than the allure of riches. By doing so, Prophet Muhammad sought to distinguish sincere believers from opportunistic followers who might compromise the mission's integrity.

Prophet Muhammad needed a cohesive group of devout followers, leading to a tactical decision to launch the Khaybar expedition with a relatively small but dedicated force. This adherence to this principle illustrated a commitment to transcending mere material gain. It stressed that war must be waged for the defense of faith or liberty, in line with the Quran's teachings.

Often, Western historians depict jihad as a war for booty. The Quran prohibits such practices. Men of true faith do not sacrifice their lives for temporary material things. Life's eternal rewards are the hope of the faithful, a concept difficult to grasp for materialistic minds. These historians tend to ignore or underestimate high morale and faith power as the key to Muslim victories in battles.

The Element of Surprise and Tactical Success

The campaign against Khaybar showcased Prophet Muhammad's strategic genius, particularly through the element of surprise. Achieving rapid mobilization, his forces moved swiftly to catch the Jewish defenses off guard, allowing them to overcome the fortified positions with considerable ease. The swift advance into Khaybar and the subsequent capture of fortifications exemplified the effectiveness of surprise in military strategy. It also demonstrated the unpreparedness of enemy forces, which had been lulled into complacency by their numerical advantage. Khaybar's hostile Jews had more than 10,000 fighters, only 90 miles from Medina.

Before the outbreak of hostilities, he extended a peace initiative to the leadership of Khaybar, underlining his role as a reconciliator rather than merely a conqueror. His letter to the Khaybar Jews framed the conflict not only in terms of military action but also in theological discourse. He identified himself as a "friend and brother of Moses."

Conclusion

The outcome of the Battle of Khaybar represented not only a tactical victory for the Prophet but also a vital turning point in the consolidation of Islamic authority and governance policies regarding Jews under Muslim rule. The negotiated settlement with Khaybar's Jews, permitting them to remain in their homeland while paying taxes, reflected a nuanced approach that balanced power with diplomacy.

Thus, the events surrounding Khaybar initiate critical reflections on the wider implications of conflict, justice, and mercy as they relate to Islam's foundational principles, allowing modern observers to rethink the circumstances under which historical events are recorded and remembered. The reconciliation efforts at Khaybar serve as reminders that Islam's core tenets advocate for coexistence and mutual respect, even amidst conflict. In this light, Khaybar's conquest was not about land, wealth, or power. Instead, it was a decisive step in the establishment of a community predicated on mercy and justice for all, irrespective of their faith.

CALL FOR UNITY AND PEACE

CHAPTER 14

A CASE FOR JEWISH HOMELAND THE HISTORY OF THE PERSECUTION OF JEWS

Jews have suffered for thousands of years, mostly from Pagan Romans and Christians and sometimes in Muslim lands. Today, the worldwide Jewish population is about 15 million, and roughly 7 million live in Israel.

From the Babylonian Captivity to the Roman Conquest

The Sack of Jerusalem by Nebuchadnezzar (587 BC): Following Nebuchadnezzar's sack of Jerusalem, the Kingdom of Judah was effectively destroyed. Most of its elite population, including the Davidic dynasty, were exiled to Babylon, marking the start of the "Babylonian Captivity" period in Jewish history. The city itself was left in ruins, and the Temple of Solomon was demolished. This led to a major shift in Jewish religious practice as they were forced to rely on scripture rather than temple rituals. While some Jews assimilated into Babylonian culture, others maintained their identity. This laid the groundwork for the later return to Zion and rebuilding of the Temple under Persian rule after Babylon fell to Cyrus the Great.

Pompey's Attack Upon Judea

Roman rule over Judea began in 63 BC after a centuries-long struggle over the blending of Greek culture and Jewish tradition exploded into civil war. Pompey, the Roman general attacked Jerusalem in 66 BC. After a three-year siege, the city surrendered and Pompey annexed Judea to Roman rule. The ramifications of this annexation were profound, as Roman authority imposed foreign governance upon the Jewish people. This established a precedent of exploitation and religious insensitivity.

Titus' Siege of Jerusalem

The zenith of Roman-Jewish conflicts occurred in 70 CE with General Titus' siege of Jerusalem, which followed the failed Great Jewish Revolt. Titus led a campaign to besiege and destroy Jerusalem, with heavy casualties. The consequences of this conquest were catastrophic. Josephus, a first-century Jewish historian, estimated that over a million people died during the siege or were sold into slavery, effectively decimating the Jewish population in Jerusalem. The destruction of the Second Temple not only marked the end of Temple-centered worship but also initiated a paradigm shift in Jewish religious practice. This paved the way for a new Judaism rooted in rabbinical teachings and community engagement.

Hadrian's Persecution of the Jews

Hadrian's persecution of Jews in 136 CE further exemplified Roman persecution. The aftermath of the Revolt—a last-ditch effort to achieve independence—resulted in Hadrian's brutal crackdown, which included selling captured Jews into slavery and abolishing Torah teaching. Synagogues were replaced with pagan Roman temples, and Jewish religious practices were severely curtailed.

Persecution of Jews under Christianity

The persecution of Jews under Christian authorities is a tragic chapter in history. It includes religious animosity, socio-political strife, and explicit persecution manifesting itself from theological disputes to violent acts. The consequences of anti-Semitism in Christian contexts illustrate a trajectory of oppression that ultimately reached horrifying heights during the Holocaust.

Blaming Jews for the Crucifixion of Jesus

Early Christians, including Paul, sought to distinguish their beliefs from Judaism, often blaming Jews collectively for Jesus' crucifixion. This accusation created a theological basis for animosity. It suggested that Jews not only rejected Christ but also maintained a legacy of guilt for his death that would carry on into future generations. Such notions became embedded in Christian doctrine, leading to the widespread belief among Christians that Jews were eternally culpable for Jesus' death, a belief that fostered subsequent prejudice and discrimination. From the 4th century onward, as Christianity became the state religion of the Roman Empire under Theodosius I, measures against Jews intensified. It led to discriminatory laws that undermined Jews' social and civil rights. This institutionalization of anti-Judaism manifested itself in various forms, including forced conversions, expulsions, and violence directed at Jewish communities across Europe.

[The Quran contradicts the popular belief that the Jews crucified Christ: *"Their boast [referring to the Jews], 'We have slain the Christ Jesus, son of Mary, [who claimed to be] an apostle of Allah!' However, they did not slay him, nor did they crucify him, but it only seemed to them so." (4:157)*]

Christian eschatology further fueled antisemitism. The belief that Jews would be left in the wake of divine judgment fueled a perspective that viewed them as a malign force within society. This perception morphed into systemic exclusion and violence, exemplifying a deadly combination of race and creed-based hatred that increasingly defined Western relations with Jewish communities.

The Medieval Era of Persecution

Crusades: Beginning in 1096, the First Crusade was accompanied by a wave of violence against Jewish communities in France and the Holy Roman Empire. Notable events included the Rhineland massacres where thousands of Jews were killed. Accusations of ritual murder, known as blood libel, portray Jews as malevolent figures preying upon Christian innocents, further exacerbating the climate of hatred and violence.

The Black Death: During the mid-14th century, Jewish communities were scapegoated and blamed for the plague. The devastation wrought by the plague saw the destruction of many Jewish communities under the false pretense that they had poisoned wells, leading to widespread violence against them.

The Inquisition further compounded Jewish suffering in Christian territories, leading to rapid and brutal forced conversions. It also executed those suspected of practicing Judaism clandestinely. Notably, in the 15th century, the expulsion of Jews from Spain marked one of the most significant and devastating moments in Jewish history. This resulted in mass migrations and diasporas.

Martin Luther and the Reformation

The Reformation in the 16th century brought another dimension to the relationship between Judaism and Christianity through Martin Luther. Initially, Luther expressed sympathy toward Jews, hoping they would convert to his vision of Christianity. However, as their responses disappointed him, he turned to vehement anti-Jewish rhetoric which culminated in his writings such as "On the Jews and Their Lies." He encouraged Jewish persecution, calling for the burning of their synagogues. It embedded anti-Semitic sentiments deeply within Protestant ideology and opened doors for future oppressions.

Modern Anti-Semitism and the Holocaust

The 19th and 20th centuries saw the evolution of traditional anti-Judaism into a more secular form of anti-Semitism, influenced by political and economic hardship. As newly unified nation-states emerged, Jews were often used as scapegoats for societal woes, manifesting themselves in violent pogroms and restrictive laws. The culmination of these longstanding prejudices reached its peak in the atrocities of the Holocaust, where Nazi ideology grotesquely intertwined traditional Christian anti-Judaism with racially based anti-Semitism. This legacy of centuries-long demonization of Jews created a moral landscape where millions were deemed expendable, leading to horrific realities of concentration camps and mass murder. Jewish sources say six million Jews were exterminated.

JEWISH PERSECUTION UNDER ISLAM

Muslim Conquest and the Salvation of Jews

David J. Wasserstein, Professor of History and Jewish Studies, stated in a seminar: "In the early seventh century C.E., Judaism was in crisis. In the Mediterranean basin, it was battered by legal, social, and religious pressure, weak in numbers, and culturally almost non-existent. It was also largely cut off from the Persian Empire's Jewry in Babylon, present-day Iraq. The future seemed clear: extinction in the West, decline to obscurity in the East. Salvation came from Arabia. Islam conquered the entire Persian Empire and most of the Mediterranean world. Uniting virtually all Jews in a single state gave them legal and religious respectability, economic and social freedoms, and linguistic and cultural conditions. This made possible a major renaissance of Judaism and the Jews."

Historically, during persecution waves in medieval Europe, many Jews found refuge in Muslim lands. Jews in Islamic lands have historically been granted the status of dhimma. This conferred upon them certain protections as "people of the book" in exchange for their subordination and acceptance of a sometimes discriminatory legal framework.

The Golden Age of Spain's Jewry

The "Golden Age of Jewry in Spain" refers to a period during Muslim Spain's rule, known as Al-Andalus, when Jewish people experienced significant religious freedom, cultural flourishing, and intellectual advancement. This period generally spans from the 8th to the 12th centuries. This era was marked by tolerance and allowed Jews to thrive in various fields like philosophy, medicine, and science. Jews were granted religious freedom and could participate actively in society, holding positions in government, scholarship, and commerce. Moses Maimonides, a prominent Jewish philosopher, is considered one of the most important figures from this era. The period of tolerance gradually declined with political instability, leading to the Jews' expulsion from Spain in 1492 by Spanish Christians.

In his discussion of "Muslim Spain," Uri Avnery, Israeli author, former Knesset member, and founder of the Gush Shalom Peace Movement, called it a "paradise for the Jews." He wrote: "There has never been a Jewish Holocaust in Muslim countries." Even pogroms were extremely rare. Prophet Muhammad decreed that 'the Peoples of the Book' be treated equally, subject to conditions more liberal than in contemporary Europe."

Granada Massacre

While Jewish communities often experienced relative stability and opportunities for cultural and economic flourishing during certain periods, they were frequently subjected to harsh restrictions and occasional bouts of violence. Notably, the 1066 Granada massacre serves as a poignant example of violence tied to the perception of Jewish political strength and social advancement, which incited anti-Semitic riots. However, it was a neighboring Muslim ruler who helped the besieged Jews.

Almohad Dynasty

Under the Almohad the Berber dynasty in the 12th century, Jews faced forced conversions and atrocities, including massacres. **The Cult of Almohadism** was founded by Ibn Tumart with his radical interpretation of God's unity or oneness. Ibn Tumart proclaimed himself to be the Mehdi or false Messiah, proclaiming extremist ideologies like ISIS of our time. Almohads rejected the status of Dhimma against the teachings of the Quran. There was a major departure from earlier Muslim governments' social policies and attitudes. The Almohads ordered Jews and Christians, the mainstream Sunni, and Shias of the Muslim majority—to accept Almohad Islam, depart, or risk death.

Comparative Analysis of Persecution

When comparing Jews' experiences under Islam and Christianity, several notable contrasts emerge.

- Firstly, the framework of legal protections provided to Jews under Islamic rule, albeit imperfectly applied, often included the status of dhimma. This recognized Jews as a protected class with some legal rights. In contrast, Christian governance often sought to marginalize Jews entirely, stripping them of legal rights and relegating them to social outcasts.
- The systematic nature of Christian oppression appears to contrast sharply with the episodic and politically contingent nature of violence experienced by Jews under Muslim rule.
- Moreover, the perception of Jews as a theological threat was more pronounced within Christianity, leading to a drive for separation and enmity. Muslims historically viewed Jews more as allies in their shared monotheistic traditions. This theological relationship fostered environments that allowed coexistence.

The conclusion drawn by historian Mark R. Cohen is that while Jews in Islamic lands occasionally faced violence, such persecution was not systematic nor as ubiquitous as in Christian Europe, suggesting that Muslim-Jewish relations were often contingent upon political circumstances.

UNDERSTANDING ANTISEMITISM

Antisemitism, often characterized as "the most ancient hatred," has deep historical roots and has manifested itself in various forms throughout the centuries. This chapter examines the origins of antisemitism, its expressions in Christian and Islamic contexts, and the contemporary implications of these historical frameworks. The thesis pursued here is that while antisemitism has been informed by theological and political contexts specific to Christianity and Islam, it is essential to understand these pathways to dismantle prejudices and seek more equitable coexistence in the modern world.

Historical Roots of Antisemitism

Antisemitism emerged from the intersection of theological beliefs and sociopolitical dynamics during Christianity's rise. The fervent belief that Jews were responsible for Jesus Christ's crucifixion laid the groundwork for anti-Jewish sentiment within Christian doctrine. This deicide charge fostered a narrative of collective guilt, embedding antisemitism within Western theological discourse. It also associated it with the broader theme of racial and economic enmity. As Christianity flourished, particularly after the second century, its rejection of Judaism as a living religion necessitated the Jewish dispossession of historical narratives.

Antisemitism in Islamic Contexts

Conversely, Islam, at its inception, shared many theological underpinnings with Judaism and initially embraced Jews as "People of the Book." The Quranic verses celebrate their historical role and divine favor. However, the establishment of Israel in 1948 drastically altered Muslim perceptions of Jews. This prompted a confluence of political and emotional responses rooted in the geopolitical turmoil surrounding the Israeli-Palestinian conflict.

The birth of modern antisemitism in some Islamic factions stems from the political ramifications of Israel's establishment. This is viewed by many as an act of colonial aggression against Palestinians. It has led to a brand of antisemitism that is often more politically motivated, emerging as a reaction to perceived injustices rather than being characterized by theological dogma seen in parts of Christianity.

Moreover, the infusion of European antisemitic tropes into Islamic discourse demonstrates a troubling overlap that undermines Islam's egalitarian tenets. For many Muslims, selective interpretations of the Quran have turned historical animosities into contemporary prejudices. This is done by disregarding passages that honor the Jewish people's significant role in monotheism.

Theological Contexts and Misinterpretations

Despite the historical coexistence depicted in early Islamic texts, current chapters in the Quran that criticize specific actions of Jewish tribes have been misappropriated by certain factions. This has fostered anti-Jewish sentiments. Such selective quotation distorts the Quran's broader message of religious tolerance and respect. The Prophet Muhammad's acknowledgment of Abraham's descendants, which encompass both Jews and Arabs, highlights Islam's inclusive nature and its core ethical tenets of equality and shared humanity.

These misconceptions provide a breeding ground for modern antisemitism—an irony, given that Islam was conceived in a milieu that celebrated Jews' monotheistic heritage and shared lineage. The historical challenges faced by Jews in predominantly Muslim societies did not reach the systematic genocides seen in Europe. This indicates that periods of relative peace have historically been possible.

Conclusion

In conclusion, the historical narratives surrounding antisemitism have been significantly shaped by theological interpretations within Christianity and the sociopolitical dynamics of the Islamic world. To create a peaceful existence, it is vital for individuals of all religious backgrounds to pursue a narrative that embraces equality, challenges biases, and collectively addresses the grievances of the past. Only by acknowledging our shared histories can we hope to overcome the enduring legacy of hatred and build a more harmonious future.

CHAPTER 15

ISLAMOPHOBIA
ITS ORIGINS, IMPACT, AND FUTURE CHALLENGES

Islamophobia, often defined as irrational fear or hostility towards Islam and its followers, has evolved into a pervasive social issue in contemporary society. This phenomenon is characterized not only by individual prejudices but also by systemic discrimination against Muslims and Islam as a religion. Islamophobia's roots are complex and can be traced through historical events and cultural narratives that have shaped perceptions of Islam. Ultimately, addressing Islamophobia requires a comprehensive understanding of its origins, manifestations, and implications for both individuals and societies.

Historical Origins of Islamophobia

Islamophobia originated in medieval Europe when the expansion of Islamic societies threatened Christian dominion, leading to various forms of hostility and animosity. Crucial moments, such as the Crusades and the Reconquista, crystallized an inherent distrust of Islam, often depicting it as a monolithic and antagonistic entity. Over the centuries, these perceptions were reinforced by anti-Muslim sentiments that emerged during significant geopolitical events, including the rise of the Ottoman Empire and encounters with colonial powers. Such historical legacies lay the groundwork for contemporary Islamophobic attitudes, which often portray Muslims as violent extremists or passive recipients of patriarchal cultures.

The landscape of Islamophobia transformed dramatically following September 11, 2001, when Muslim identity became inextricably linked with the narrative of terrorism in the United States and abroad. Since then, negative media portrayals have often conflated Islam with acts of violence, perpetuating stereotypes that undergird systematic Islamophobia. This environment has fostered a public perception that is not only hostile but legitimizes discriminatory policies against Muslim communities. This is reflecting a broader pattern of xenophobia and racism.

Manifestations of Islamophobia

Islamophobia manifests itself in various ways, including hate crimes, discrimination, and legislative actions targeting Muslim individuals and communities. Data suggests that hate crimes against Muslims have surged in the post-9/11 era. This reflects a society that increasingly stigmatizes and alienates individuals based on their religious identity. The FBI reported that hate crimes against Muslims were five times more common after the September 11 attacks. It attributed this rise to Muslims' increased visibility and a corresponding spike in anti-Muslim rhetoric in political and social discourse.

Moreover, structural Islamophobia is present within institutional frameworks, influencing various sectors including law enforcement, education, and healthcare. For instance, policies such as the Patriot Act, which disproportionately targeted Muslim communities under the guise of national security, have fostered an environment of fear and suspicion. This systemic discrimination not only marginalizes Muslims but also negatively impacts their mental health and overall well-being, as social stigma interferes with community bonds and the ability to seek help and access resources.

Islamophobia's Impact on Muslim Communities

Islamophobia's implications reach far beyond mere prejudice; they affect Muslim communities' social fabric and health. Ongoing studies highlight the psychological toll associated with living in a climate of fear and hostility. This can lead to increased stress, anxiety, and depression among Muslims. Children, particularly, suffer from faith-based bullying, exacerbating isolation and insecurity in school environments. The intersection of Islamophobic attitudes with racial and ethnic identity also creates unique challenges for individuals who belong to marginalized racial groups. This complicates their social experiences and health outcomes.

Furthermore, Islamophobia can fuel an array of discriminatory practices, from verbal harassment to physical violence. This impacts not only the Muslim community but society at large. Hate crimes, often overlooked or downplayed in media narratives, demonstrate a disturbing trend where Muslim individuals' security and dignity are routinely compromised. This reinforces a cycle of fear that disincentivizes engagement between communities and promotes divisions based on unfounded fears and stereotypes.

Addressing Islamophobia: A Path Forward

Combating Islamophobia necessitates a multi-faceted approach that encompasses education, community engagement, and policy reform. Educational initiatives aimed at dismantling stereotypes surrounding Islam and promoting interfaith dialogue can help mitigate negative perceptions. Furthermore, public awareness campaigns that highlight Muslims' contributions to society can help reshape narratives and showcase the diversity within Muslim communities. This will counter prevalent monolithic portrayals.

On a policy level, concerted efforts must be made to counter structural Islamophobia through legislative measures that protect Muslims' rights and promote inclusivity across all facets of society. Given the intertwined nature of racial and religious discrimination, it is crucial to foster environments where equality and acceptance prevail. This will ensure that all individuals can navigate their identities without fear of backlash or harm.

Conclusion

Islamophobia is a multifaceted issue that requires a nuanced understanding of its historical origins, manifestations, and significant impacts on Muslim communities. By addressing the root causes and challenging the narratives that perpetuate fear and hatred towards Islam and Muslims, society can work towards building a more inclusive world. Ultimately, combating Islamophobia is not solely a concern for Muslims; it is a critical issue for society, reflecting our collective commitment to dignity, respect, and human rights for all individuals, regardless of their faith or background. Through education, advocacy, and solidarity, society can strive to dismantle Islamophobia barriers, fostering a future marked by mutual understanding and acceptance.

CHAPTER 16

THE DIVINE LAW OF DIVERSITY

The notion of diversity as an intrinsic element of divine intention is articulated through the principle that God's revelations are tailor-made to meet the needs of humanity across different eras and societies. This premise responds to critiques often posed by adherents of other faiths, who argue that the variations found within the Quran compared to earlier scriptures invalidate either the Quran or the scriptures it succeeds. In fact, such differences do not inherently undermine the truth of divine messages; rather, they underscore God's will to suit various audiences throughout history.

Diversity is the essence of life

Diversity permeates every aspect of existence, from countless human traits to nature's myriad differences. No two individuals are the same, and even among the trillions of leaves on trees, each displays unique characteristics. This vast array of diversity—racial, religious, cultural, and linguistic—demonstrates God's infinite wisdom. In acknowledging this multiplicity, we recognize that diversity not only enriches the human experience but also exemplifies God's creative genius.

The Origin of Humanity from One Living Entity

The Quran emphasizes humanity's common origin, asserting that all people descend from one living entity, supported by the following verse: *O mankind! Be conscious of your Sustainer, who created you from one living entity. Out of it created its mate, and out of the two spawned a multitude of men and women. (4:1) It is He who created you [all] out of one living entity and brought its mate. (7:189) Now had God so willed, He could surely have made them all one community. (42:8)* The implication is that God has not willed humanity to be a single community. This fundamental truth highlights our shared lineage, which ultimately fosters kinship among all people. The verses remind us that divisions based on race, caste, or creed are contrary to God's design. His intention was for humanity to embody unity amidst diversity.

Intellectual Development and Divine Guidance

As humanity evolved, so did its societies, transitioning from primitive homogeneity to complex structures that necessitated divine guidance. The initial consensus in thought and behavior split as individuals sought to redefine morality and justice, leading to distinct moral codes. The Quran delineates this transition: *All humanity was once one single community [then they began to differ]. After that, God raised the prophets as heralds of glad tidings and warners. Through them He bestowed revelation from on high, setting forth the truth. So that it might decide between people with divergent views. (2:213)* This divergence introduced the need for prophets who conveyed divine messages tailored to the evolving moral landscape. Here, the Quran indicates that humanity has a God-given prerogative to grapple with diverse opinions as a path toward enlightenment and self-discovery.

The Nature of Intellectual Dissent

The Quran acknowledges the inevitability of intellectual dissent, as illustrated in the assertion that *"If God had so intended, they who succeeded those [apostles] would not have contended after all evidence of the truth had come to them. But [as it was], they took to divergent views. Yet if God had so willed, they would not have contended, but God does whatever He wills." (2:253)*

This acknowledgment posits intellectual disagreement not as an aberration but as an essential characteristic of human nature, divinely ordained for thought and understanding progression. Through this lens, dissent is a catalyst for cultural and personal development. It challenges existing norms and fosters a richer dialogue about values and beliefs.

Diversity in Colors, Languages, and Sexes

Human diversity manifests itself not only in ethnic and cultural variation but also in the kaleidoscope of individual expression and interaction. As stated in the Quran, *"His wonders are this: He creates you out of dust, and then, lo! You become a human being that reaches far and wide! And among his wonders are the diversity of your tongues and colors. For in this, there are messages for all who possess [innate] knowledge!" (30:20-22)* Such diversity serves essential ecological and social functions, fostering resilience among populations and enhancing adaptability amidst changing environmental conditions. Any form of racism or discrimination contradicts the divine narrative of unity, as God's intention was for humanity to reflect a harmonious multiplicity.

Diversity in Worship

The various worship paths upheld by different communities are another testament to divine diversity. The Quran articulates this ethos, stating, *"Unto every community, We have appointed [different] ways of worship, which they ought to observe. Hence, [O believer], do not let those [who follow paths other than yours] draw you into disputes on this score." (22:67)* This diversity of worship underscores the importance of tolerance in religious practice, inviting believers to understand that a variety of expressions of faith can coexist and flourish. It calls on followers to engage with one another respectfully and recognize that their shared commitment to God transcends their differing worship methods.

Common Spiritual Truth and the Quran's Validity

The Quran also posits a shared spiritual truth across various divine revelations. It suggests that while time and context may reshape revelation's form, the core message remains consistent. As expressed in verse 10:94-97: *"And so, [O man], if you are in doubt about [the truth of] what We have [now] bestowed upon you from on high, ask those who read the divine writ [revealed] before your time. [You will find that] surely; the truth has now come unto you from thy Sustainer."*

Individuals are encouraged to seek wisdom from those versed in previous scriptures to bridge any understanding gaps. Thus, the Quran serves not as a dismissal of earlier truths, but as a culmination of divine messages designed to guide humanity toward a more profound comprehension of their faith.

Conclusion

The divine law of diversity is a robust framework that illustrates God's multifaceted design for humanity's existence. The Quran, along with earlier revelations, emphasizes that while differences in belief and practice may arise, they do not invalidate the truth of divine guidance. Instead, these differences enrich the human experience, fostering tolerance and respect among diverse populations. As humanity navigates the complexities of moral and intellectual development, it is this diversity that ultimately reflects God's profound nature. The essence of an inclusive society rests on the recognition and celebration of this diversity, as it honors divine intent interwoven into the very fabric of human life.

CHAPTER 17

COMMON BELIEFS AMONG JEWS, CHRISTIANS, AND MUSLIMS

The three primary monotheistic faiths—Judaism, Christianity, and Islam—share a multitude of foundational beliefs that unite them more than they differentiate them. While societal narratives often emphasize their differences, a deeper analysis reveals that these faiths are intertwined through a common spiritual heritage rooted in mutual values, beliefs about God, and prophetic traditions. This chapter elucidates these shared beliefs and their significance as outlined in the Quran. This promotes unity rather than division among these faiths.

The Oneness of God

Do not argue with the followers of earlier revelation otherwise than in a most kindly manner and say: "We believe in that which has been bestowed from on high upon us, and that which has been bestowed upon you: for our God and your God is one and the same, and it is unto Him that We [all] surrender ourselves." (29:46-47)

Central to Judaism, Christianity, and Islam is the belief in a singular, omnipotent God. The Quran explicitly underlines this commonality, asserting that both Muslims and the adherents of earlier revelations worship the same God. As stated, *"And it is unto Him that we [all] surrender ourselves."* This shared understanding fosters respectful dialogue among religions, encouraging followers to recognize that their diverse paths lead to the same divine source. Furthermore, the Quran commands believers not to engage in disputes about God except in a kind and respectful manner, emphasizing the need for mutual acknowledgment of each faith's devotion to the one God.

The recognition of God as the eternal sustainer, transcending cultural and linguistic differences, is also highlighted by the Quran. Phrases like *"My prayer, and [all] my acts of worship, and my living and my dying are for God [alone]"(6:162)* reflect this commitment to divine oneness, reinforcing the idea that despite their varied practices and beliefs, faith remains directed toward the same Deity.

Shared Prophetic Traditions

We bestowed upon him [Abraham] Isaac and Jacob, and We guided each of them as We had instructed Noah aforetime. And out of his offspring, [We bestowed prophethood upon] David, Solomon, Job, Joseph, Moses, and Aaron. Thus, We reward the doers of good. And [upon] Zachariah, John, Jesus, and Elijah, everyone was righteous, and [upon] Ishmael, Elisha, Jonah, and Lot. [We exalted] some of their forefathers, offspring, and brethren. We elected them [all] and guided them on the straight way and such is God's guidance. We vouchsafe revelation, sound judgment, and prophethood for them. (6:84-89) Another significant commonality lies in the prophetic traditions that are revered across these religions. Figures such as Abraham, Moses, and Jesus hold revered positions for Christians and Muslims, each viewed as a conduit for God's message to humanity. The Quran cites numerous prophets and insists that they were all sent to guide people on the straight path of righteousness. The parable of the three prophets—Moses, Jesus, and Muhammad—illustrates that these figures embody the same divine truth, addressing moral dilemmas faced by their communities in different yet complementary manners.

The Quran further reminds believers of the shared legacy of these prophets, emphasizing that moral and ethical teachings remain essentially the same across these faiths. This creates interconnectedness, suggesting not only a historical continuum but also a mutual responsibility to uphold the virtues they espouse.

Reverence for the Holy Texts

And yet, before this, there was the revelation of Moses, a guide and a [manifestation of God's] grace. This [Quran] is a divine writ confirming the truth [of the Torah]. (46:12)

The concept of sacred texts underlines another layer of commonality between the three religions. Each faith regards its scriptures—the Torah for Jews, the Gospel for Christians, and the Quran for Muslims—as divine revelations guiding their adherents. The Quran acknowledges previous scriptures, stating, *"He who has bestowed from on high the Torah and the Gospel" (3:3)* serves as guidance for humanity.

Moreover, the Quran calls upon its readers to respect the divine revelations bestowed upon earlier communities. It recognizes the foundational significance of these texts in shaping moral frameworks and spiritual beliefs. This acknowledgment of shared sacred texts promotes respectful exchange among faith communities and validates each religious tradition's unique contributions.

Sanctity of Places of Worship

The Quran emphasizes the sanctity and respect owed to places of worship of all faiths. It acknowledges churches, synagogues, and mosques as the houses of God, deserving of protection and reverence. The text highlights that these places serve as sanctuaries for believers attempting to connect with the divine. It also admonishes individuals who prevent others from worshipping in these sanctuaries. *If God had not enabled people to defend themselves against one another, [all] monasteries, churches, synagogues and mosques in which God's name is abundantly extolled—would surely have been destroyed [before now]. (22:40) Hence, who could be more wicked than those who bar God's name from His houses of worship? (2:114)*

This respect for religious diversity enters the broader ethical discourse of interfaith relations, urging followers to understand and engage with one another's beliefs thoughtfully. It illustrates that the act of worship, regardless of its specific form, is fundamentally a commendable pursuit for all three faiths.

Conclusion

In conclusion, the foundational beliefs shared among Jews, Christians, and Muslims, as outlined in the Quran, reveal a significant commonality that transcends mere doctrinal differences. Recognition of a singular God, a lineage of revered prophets, respect for sacred texts, and acknowledgment of the sanctity of all houses of worship converge to illustrate that these three monotheistic faiths are less disparate than they are united in their spiritual essence. In a world often characterized by conflict and division, embracing these similarities is essential for fostering dialogue, understanding, and peace among adherents of different faiths. By focusing on what unites rather than divides, followers of these traditions can work towards a future grounded in mutual respect and collaboration.

CHAPTER 18

WHAT DID JESUS SAY ABOUT SALVATION?

In the Gospels, Jesus lays down the principles of universal salvation based on good deeds, repentance, and sin forgiveness. Salvation is not restricted to denominations or religious affiliations.

Lord's Prayer: Forgiveness Begets Forgiveness

Today, give us our daily bread and forgive us for our sins, as we have forgiven those who sin against us. If you forgive others when they sin against you, your heavenly Father will also forgive you. But if you refuse to forgive others, your Father will not forgive your sins. (Matthew 6:5-15)

Forgiveness is the central theme of the Lord's prayer. God will then forgive our sins as we forgive others who sin against us. The concept is identical to the Quran's teachings.

The Salvation of the Poor and the Wealthy

According to Jesus, the meek, the poor, those who thirst after righteousness, those who are persecuted for righteousness, those who are pure of heart, merciful, peacemakers, etc., will enter the Kingdom of God. Contrast that with what Jesus said about the salvation of the wealthy. (See next).

Dialogue With a Wealthy Young Man

As Jesus walked, a man ran up to him and fell on his knees before him. "Good teacher," he asked, "what must I do to inherit eternal life?" "Why do you call me good?" Jesus answered. "No one is good—except God alone." "You know the commandment: 'You shall not murder, you shall not commit adultery, you shall not steal, you shall not give false testimony, you shall not defraud, honor your father and mother. "Teacher," he declared, "all these I have kept since I was a boy." Jesus looked at him and loved him. "One thing you lack is," He said, "Go sell everything you have and give to the poor, and you will have treasure in heaven. Then come, follow me." At this, the man's face fell. He walked away disappointed because he had substantial wealth.

"Why do you call me good? Only God is good." Jesus emphasizes his humanness and vulnerability. Jesus only mentioned commandments relating to fellow men's rights, stressing orthopraxy (deeds) over orthodoxy (correct beliefs).

Jesus looked around and said to his disciples, "It is easier for a camel (rope in some translations) *to go through the eye of a needle than for someone rich to enter the kingdom of God." The disciples were even more amazed and questioned, "Who then can be saved?" Jesus looked at them and answered, "With man, this is impossible, but not with God; all things are possible with God." (Mark 10:17-31)*

Leading a righteous life and doing righteous deeds exemplify a good-faith effort. While good deeds alone may not save people (with man, it's impossible). By God's grace and mercy, eternal life is possible.

Repentance and Restoring Victims' Usurped Rights

Jesus encountered a man named Zacchaeus a wealthy chief tax collector. Zacchaeus said to Jesus, "Half of my possessions I will give to the poor, and if I have defrauded anyone of anything, I will give back four times as much." And Jesus said to him, "Today salvation has come to this house because he too is a son of Abraham." (Luke 19:5-10)

For true repentance of sins against a fellow man, one must restore usurped rights and ask forgiveness from the victim and God. Most importantly, not to repeat the same sin again. This is consistent with

Quranic teachings. The goal is to become better by learning from mistakes and being a better person than before.

All the prophets in the Kingdom

In that place, there will be weeping and gnashing of teeth when you see Abraham, Isaac, and Jacob, and all the prophets in the kingdom of God. However, you were cast out. And people will come from east and west, north and south, and sit down at the table in God's kingdom. And behold, some are last who will be first, and some are first who will be last." (Luke 13:28–30)

The Fate of the Sheep and the Goats

"When the Son of Man comes in his glory, and all the angels are with him, he will sit on his glorious throne. All the nations will be gathered before him, and he will separate the people as a shepherd separates the sheep from the goats. He will put the sheep on his right and the goats on his left.

Sheep on the Right (Commission of Good Deeds)

"Then the King will say to those on his right, 'Come, you who are blessed by my Father; take your inheritance. The kingdom has been prepared for you since the world was created. For I was hungry, and you gave me something to eat. I was thirsty, and you gave me something to drink. I was a stranger, and you invited me in. I needed clothes, and you clothed me. I was sick, and you looked after me. I was in prison, and you visited me.' "Then the righteous will answer him, 'Lord, when did we see you hungry and feed you, or thirsty and give you something to drink? When did we see you as a stranger and invite you in, or need clothes and clothe you? When did you become sick or in prison and visit you?' "The King will reply, 'Truly I tell you, whatever you did for one of the least of these brothers and sisters of mine, you did for me.'

Goats on the Left (Omission of Good Deeds)

"Then he will say to those on his left, 'Depart from me, you cursed ones, into the eternal fire prepared for the devil and his angels. For I was hungry, and you gave me nothing to eat, I was thirsty, and you gave me nothing to drink, I was a stranger, and you did not invite me in. I needed clothes, and you did not clothe me. I was sick and in prison, and you did not look after me.' "They also will answer, 'Lord, when did we see you hungry or thirsty or a stranger or needing clothes or sick or in prison, and did not help you?' "He will reply, 'Truly I tell you, whatever you did not do for one of the least of these, you did not do for me.' "Then they will go away to eternal punishment, but the righteous to eternal life." (Matthew 25:31-46)

In this spectacular passage, Jesus makes it crystal clear that people will be saved not because they believe in Christ. They will enter paradise because they helped people in need. Salvation is based on good deeds, not just belief. It is in line with the Quranic teachings. In addition, salvation is not restricted to denominations or religious affiliations.

CHAPTER 19

THE UNIVERSAL DOCTRINE OF SALVATION

The concept of salvation has been a central tenet in many religious traditions, associated with divine favor and alleviation of suffering. Among these traditions, salvation doctrines in Islam, Judaism, and Christianity display both shared principles and unique characteristics. These doctrines illustrate their perspectives on righteousness and unity. This chapter explores salvation doctrines as understood by these faiths. It will focus on the commonalities and the imperative for unity amidst diversity, as reflected in both Quranic teachings and biblical texts.

Common Foundations of Salvation

The Quran articulates a comprehensive understanding of salvation that extends across religious boundaries. The Quran emphasizes that righteous individuals from diverse faith backgrounds—Muslims, Jews, Christians, and Sabians—can attain God's reward by believing in Him and performing good deeds. Such inclusivity that underlines salvation doctrine resonates with the essence of God's mercy. The shared conviction that belief in a single God, adherence to ethical conduct, and the pursuit of righteousness are fundamental to eternal life creates interconnectedness among these three major faiths.

Unitarian Faiths Versus Idol Worship

"As for those who have attained faith [in this divine writ] [such as Muslims], and those who follow the Jewish faith, the Sabians, the Christians, and the Magians, [on the one hand], and those who are bent on ascribing divinity to aught

but God, [on the other] verily, God will decide between them on Resurrection Day: for, behold, God is the witness unto everything." (22:17)

Zoroaster's followers (Magians) and Christians are included in the Unitarian faith, along with Jews, Muslims, and Sabians in verse 22:16. It is noteworthy that the Quran does not include Christians and Magians among those who attribute divinity to anything besides God. However, Christians and Magians attribute divine qualities to other beings besides God.

Christians regard those beings, fundamentally, as no more than manifestations—or incarnations—of the One God, thus persuading themselves that they worship one God alone. Their actions can only be interpreted based on their intentions.

Zoroaster's followers worship one God. Ahura Mazda is the primary deity, considered the creator and source of all good. However, it has a strong dualistic element: a constant struggle between good (Ahura Mazda) and evil (Angra Mainyu) is central to the faith.

Idol worshippers, on the other hand, are "those who deliberately ascribe divinity to beings other than God" and reject the principle of His oneness and uniqueness (22:17). God will decide their destiny with justice on the resurrection, and they will not be arbitrarily condemned.

The Three Criteria of Universal Salvation

"Those who have attained faith [in this divine writ, i.e. Muslims], and those who follow the Jewish faith, the Christians, and the Sabians—all who believe in God and the last day and do righteous deeds— shall have their reward with their Sustainer. They need not fear nor grieve." (5:69) "For those who have attained faith [in this divine writ], and those who follow the Jewish faith, the Sabians, the Christians—all who believe in God and the Last Day and do righteous deeds— no fear is needed, and neither shall they grieve." (2:62)

The Sabians seem to have been a monotheistic religious group intermediate between Judaism and Christianity. Their name (probably derived from the Aramaic verb tsebha "he immersed himself in water") indicates they were followers of John the Baptist.

Religious pluralism is the state of being where everyone in an ethnically diverse society has the rights, freedoms, and safety to worship, or not to worship, according to their conscience. The above passages occur in the Quran several times and lay down a fundamental message of pluralism and salvation.

Salvation is not restricted to Muslims because Islam is not the only way to God. Islam categorically states that people from other faiths will also ascend to heaven. It applies to Adam and the last human on this earth and is therefore of timeless import and transcends all religious affiliations. With a breadth of vision unparalleled, the idea of Quranic "salvation" is conditional upon the following three factors: belief in God, belief in the Day of Judgment, and above all, righteous actions in this life.

Faith in God is the only objective source of all moral law from which to judge the true and untrue, right and wrong. Therefore, individuals and societies are bound by ethical valuation standards.

Judgment Day—Belief in Judgment Day is accepting responsibility for one's actions and an incentive to avoid evil deeds and do virtuous works. Man controls his actions and is entirely responsible for his decisions. For Muslims, life on earth is the seedbed of an eternal future. It will be followed by a day of reckoning. Depending on how it fares in this accounting, the soul will then be sent either to Hell or Heaven.

Good Works—The belief in God and Judgment Day is a powerful motivation to do righteous deeds and avoid evil, a major cause of misery. Only through righteous acts can a better and just society be established.

God's Grace or Mercy Key to Salvation

Leading a righteous life exemplifies a good faith effort on the part of the believer. Good deeds alone will not be enough. In the end, God's mercy is the key to salvation. All human beings including the highly exalted Prophets need God's forgiveness. The Prophet said, "Act and try to act as righteously as you possibly can but know that a person's action alone will not make him enter Paradise." When asked what about your actions? He replied, "Yes, even I will not make it to paradise on the strength of my actions unless my Lord covers me up in His mercy." Two diverse pathways to salvation in Christianity and Islam have a common convergence in God's Grace or Mercy as a deciding factor in achieving eternal life.

Gift of Love

"Those who attain faith and do righteous deeds the Most Gracious will endow them with love." (19:96–97) "Those who have attained faith and done righteous deeds, We shall most certainly cause them to join the blessed [in the hereafter as well]." (29:9) "Anyone who did [whatever he could] of righteous deeds, and was a believer, need have no fear of being wronged or deprived [of any of his merit]." (20:112) "God has promised those who attain faith and do good works, theirs shall be forgiveness of sins and a mighty reward." (5:9) "We shall erase their [previous] wrongdoings and reward them for the finest they ever did." (29:7)

Self-Responsibility

"No bearer of burden shall bear another's burden." (35:18) Thus, any transfer of moral responsibility from one person to another is impossible. All wrongs committed by humans will be judged on Judgment Day. It refers to moral burdens: you can't ask someone else to absolve you of your sins. You must shoulder them yourself by repenting and repairing the damage you did.

Righteous Strive for Here and Hereafter

Those who pray, "O our Sustainer! Grant us blessings in this world and happiness in the life to come and keep us safe from suffering through fire." It is these that shall have their portion [of happiness] in return for what they have earned. (2:201-202) "God is most kind unto His creatures. He provides sustenance for whomever He wills—for He alone is powerful, almighty! To him who desires a harvest in the life to come, We will increase his harvest." (42:19-20)

Those who live righteously and turn their efforts towards spiritual ends are sure to receive in the hereafter more than they hope for. God would have made a clear-cut distinction, in this world, between those who look forward to the hereafter and those who care only about worldly success, by granting unlimited happiness to the former and causing the latter to suffer. Since man's life is only truly fulfilled in the hereafter, God has postponed this distinction until then.

Keeping a Covenant with God and Man

"Those who are true to their bond with God and never break their covenant. They keep together what God has intended to be joined. They are patient in adversity, constant in prayer, and spend on others, secretly and openly, out of what We provide for them as sustenance. They repel evil with good." (13:20-22)

The "covenant" is the spiritual obligation arising from one's faith in God and the moral and social obligations towards one's fellow men. The phrase "What God has intended to be joined" refers to all ties arising from human relationships—e.g., family bonds, responsibility for orphans and the poor, neighbors' mutual rights and duties. It also applies to the ethical and practical bonds between all who belong to Islam's brotherhood (8:75). It includes the moral duty to treat all living beings with love and compassion. They do not repay evil with evil but repel it by doing good. The end result of their patience in adversity will be the attainment of the ultimate abode or life in the hereafter.

Record of Good Works

"It is to Him that ascend all good words, and He exalts righteous deeds." (35:10) "And everything [that man does], whether small or great, is recorded [with God]." (54:53) "And [withal] We do not burden any human being with more than he can bear. For with Us is a record that speaks the truth [about what men do and can do], and none shall be wronged." (23:62)

The Weight of Righteousness Heavy in the Balance

"Whose weight [of righteousness] is heavy in the balance—it is they who will attain a happy state." (23:102) "Whereas anyone—be it man or woman—who does [whatever he can] of good deeds and is a believer, shall enter paradise, and not be wronged by as much as [would fill] the groove of a date-stone." (4:124) "Behold, [only] those who attain to faith, do righteous deeds and humble themselves before their Sustainer—[only] they are destined for paradise, and there shall they abide." (11:23)

Those Who Achieve a Happy State

"Anyone who repents and attains faith and does righteous deeds may well [hope to] find himself among those who achieve a happy state [in the life to come]." (28:67) "They will enter Paradise and will not be wronged in any way. [Theirs will be the] gardens of perpetual bliss which the Most Gracious has promised to His servants, in a realm beyond human perception: His promise is ever certain to be fulfilled!" (19:60-63) "The God-conscious will find themselves in [a paradise of] gardens and running waters, in a seat of truth, in the presence of a Sovereign who determines everything." (54:54-55)

Salvation By Observing Torah and The Gospel

"If the Bible followers attain [true] faith and God-consciousness, We should indeed erase their [previous] evil deeds, and certainly, bring them into gardens of bliss. If they truly observe the Torah, the Gospel, and all [the revelation] bestowed from on

high upon them by their Sustainer, they will certainly partake of all the blessings of heaven and earth." (5:65-66)

Christianity and salvation

Christian doctrine posits that faith in Jesus Christ is the key to salvation but also recognizes righteousness outside its confines. Christian teachings emphasize the necessity of good works alongside faith. "Grace" is a recurring theme that enables salvation for all who act righteously, as seen in biblical passages advocating mercy and compassion towards others. Thus, both traditions maintain that while doctrinal differences exist, the fundamental aim remains the same—redeeming humanity through righteousness and conduct reflective of divine will.

"Thou will surely find that, of all people, they who say, "We are Christians," come closest to feeling affection for those who hold faith [in this divine writ i.e. Muslims]. This is so because there are priests and monks among them, who are not given to arrogance. For, when they understand what has been bestowed from high upon this Apostle, thou canst see their eyes overflow with tears because they recognize something of its truth. And for this, their belief, God will reward them with gardens through which running waters flow, therein to abide; for such is the reward of the doers of good." (5:82-86)

Those Deeply Rooted in Knowledge

"But as for those among them [Jews] who are deeply rooted in knowledge, and the believers [Muslims] who believe in what has been bestowed upon thee from on high and that what was bestowed from on high before thee? Those who pray constantly, give generously in charity, believe in God and the Last Day-to whom We grant a mighty reward." (4:162) Those who are deeply rooted in knowledge do not content themselves with mere ritual observance but try to penetrate the deepest meaning of faith.

CHAPTER 20

THE TWO NATION THEORY?

The Legacy of Canaanites

The ancient Canaanites serve as a focal point for understanding contemporary Jews and Arabs' genetic and cultural lineage. Historically perceived as people inhabiting a land rich in resources until their conquest by the Israelites, recent genetic research illuminates a more complex narrative of continuity rather than disappearance. This chapter will explore modern genetic findings that affirm the ancestral connection between today's Jewish and Arab populations and the Canaanites. It will also challenge the notion of a distinct two-nation theory. Furthermore, we will examine the implications of these findings within the context of racism and the ideological complexities surrounding chosen peoples. This is especially relevant to religious and historical narratives.

Canaanites as Ancestors of Modern Populations

Recent DNA analysis has demonstrated that modern Jewish and Arabic-speaking communities are descendants of the ancient Canaanites, providing a bridge between historical and contemporary identities. A study analyzed 93 individuals' genomes, revealing that more than half of the ancestry of these modern populations can be traced back to the Canaanites. This compelling evidence contradicts centuries of historical narratives that portrayed the Canaanites as obliterated by newer populations. Instead, genetic continuity suggests a shared lineage, emphasizing that Jews and Palestinians are, biologically speaking, closer than previously understood. These findings challenge the conceptual separation of identity typically posited by political conflicts.

The Challenge to Two-Nation Theory

Genetic studies have further revealed that Y chromosome variations between Middle Eastern Arabs and Jews are nearly identical. This indicates a shared paternal lineage that transcends political and cultural boundaries. The Y chromosome, one of the sex chromosomes, is passed directly from a father to his male offspring only. This means that a male inherits his Y chromosome solely from his father. It remains largely unchanged across generations, allowing for tracing paternal lineage through genetic analysis.

Genetic data undermine the two-nation theory, which posits Jews and Palestinians as fundamentally distinct peoples with divergent ancestries. In practice, this means that the ongoing Israeli-Palestinian conflict, often framed as an ethnic or nationalist struggle, may better be understood as a cultural conflict rooted in shared genetics rather than racial differences. The two populations are not just neighbors in a land filled with historical grievances but represent two branches of the same ancient ancestry.

Reflections on Racism and Identity

Racism, defined as the belief in the inherent superiority of one racial or ethnic group over others, permeates discussions of identity across a spectrum of cultures and religions. Historical constructs of superiority often become entrenched in societal norms and lead to systemic discrimination. In the context of Jewish identity, notions of being a "chosen people" can become a basis for perceived superiority, as reflected in discriminatory attitudes towards Palestinians and other non-Jews. Gideon Levy's poignant reflections on Israeli attitudes towards Palestinians underscore the deep-seated biases that persist despite our shared genetic heritage.

Meanwhile, the concepts of chosen peoplehood within Judaism and Islam present theological and moral quandaries. For instance, Mordecai Kaplan, a notable Jewish thinker, argued against the inherent superiority implied by chosenness. He promoted a view of Judaism that recognizes shared moral responsibilities among all humanity, rather than an exclusive covenant with one ethnic group. In stark contrast, the Quran explicitly refutes notions of racial superiority, advocating equality among all humans based on righteousness and piety rather than ethnicity.

Conclusion

- Shared ancestry: Both populations are largely descended from ancient populations in the Levant, leading to high genetic overlap.
- Y chromosome similarities: Studies analyzing Y chromosomes have revealed a substantial portion of the shared genetic material between Jews and Palestinians.
- Regional variations: While genetically close, slight differences can be observed depending on specific Jewish and Palestinian subgroups and historical migration patterns.
- Impact on conflict narratives: The genetic closeness between Jews and Palestinians challenges narratives that solely attribute the Israeli-Palestinian conflict to ethnic differences.

CHAPTER 21

THE VISION OF UNITY

Division Within Communities

The tradition holds that divisions counteract the original scriptural teachings of unity. The Prophet Muhammad's anecdote regarding the multiplicity of sects among Jews, Christians, and Muslims reminds us of the importance of maintaining a cohesive faith community. The Quran condemns these divisions, urging believers to uphold the bond between God and one another. It also preserves mercy and collective accountability principles in their practices.

The divisions that have emerged across and within various faiths often obscure the core messages of compassion, righteousness, and unity. Quranic verses and Christian teachings illuminate that believers should strive to transcend sectarian barriers. They should embrace each other as brothers and sisters within one overarching faith community. The Jewish value of communal responsibility echoes this sentiment, where everyone's actions can affect the entire community's standing before God. Despite the clear call for unity, history records the splintering of various religious communities into sects.

The Quran and the Call for Equality

Islamic teachings present a radical departure from notions of hereditary superiority. The Quran states that all humans are descended from Adam and Eve, thereby establishing fundamental equality among all people. *"O mankind! We have created you from male and female and made you into nations and tribes that you may know one another." Verily, the noblest of you in God's sight is the one who is most deeply conscious of Him. Behold, God is all-knowing, all-aware." (Quran 49:13)* The verse urges recognition of shared humanity and warns against divisions based on race or ethnicity. Prophet Muhammad's final sermon underscored this egalitarian stance by declaring that no individual is superior to another based solely on their lineage or skin color. The only thing that makes them superior is their good deeds and their consciousness of God. He said: *"Humanity comes from Adam and Eve. An Arab has no superiority over a non-Arab, nor a non-Arab has any superiority over an Arab; also, a white has no superiority over a black, nor a black has any superiority over a white except through piety and virtuous actions."*

"Summon [all mankind], and pursue the right course, as you have been bidden [by God]; and do not follow their likes and dislikes but say: "I believe in whatever revelation God has bestowed from on high, and I am bidden to bring about equity in your mutual views. God is our and your Sustainer. To us shall be accounted for our deeds, and to you, your deeds. Let there be no contention between us and you: God will bring us all together—for with Him is all our journeys' end." (42:15)

The Quranic Vision of Unity

The Quran further emphasizes the notion of a unified community among believers. It states that all who faithfully worship God constitute a single collective, although their practices may vary. *"Verily, [O you who believe in Me,] this community of yours is one single community since I am the Sustainer of you all: worship, then, Me [alone]!" (21:92)* Believers are defined as those who worship one God and do not practice idolatry. This call for unity echoes throughout the scriptures, urging adherents to find common ground in their devotion to God and mutual support. Verses such as 23:52 assert that despite divisions, there exists a divine bond that connects them all. *"And this community of yours is one single community since I am the Sustainer of you all: remain, then, conscious of Me!" (23:52)* The recognition that all stem from a shared divine source fosters an environment of cooperation rather than division, an ethos that is paramount in leadership and community building as encouraged in various religious texts.

In the Jewish tradition, unity is equally important. Prophetic teachings urge Israel to remain committed to God's covenant while acting justly and upholding community bonds. This imperative for solidarity speaks to a broader theological vision of a harmonious relationship among those who share unitarian God's worship. Thus, the prophetic texts promote social justice and ethical behavior as expressions of divine will that engender unity among faith followers.

Universal Doctrine of Salvation

The Quran articulates a comprehensive understanding of salvation that extends across religious boundaries. It emphasizes that righteous individuals from diverse faith backgrounds—Muslims, Jews, Christians, Zoroastrians, and Sabians—can attain God's reward by believing in Him and performing good deeds. Such inclusivity underlines a doctrine of salvation that resonates with the essence of God's mercy. The shared conviction that belief in a single God, adherence to ethical conduct, and the pursuit of righteousness are fundamental to eternal life creates interconnectedness among these three major faiths.

Islam, Judaism, and Christianity reveal both convergence and divergence in salvation doctrines on righteousness and unity. While each faith delineates unique pathways to salvation, the essential belief in a compassionate and just God binds them through a shared moral framework. In the end, both Christian and Islamic pathways to salvation converge on God's grace. Prophet Muhammad said, *"Act and try to act as righteously as you possibly can but know that a person's action alone will not make him enter Paradise." When asked what about your actions? He replied, "Yes, even I will not make it to paradise on the strength of my actions unless my Lord covers me up in His mercy."*

As these scriptures highlight mutual respect, collective accountability remains the basis for interreligious harmony. Through dialogue and understanding, followers of these Abrahamic faiths can pursue a path of unity that enhances their worship of the one true God. This will nourish the values of mercy and righteousness at the heart of their traditions.

The Quran states: Help Enemies Become Friends

"Good and evil cannot be equal. You can combat [evil] with something better. Between you and him, what was once enmity may become as if he had always been close to you, a true friend! Yet [achieving] this is not given to anyone but those who are patient in adversity and endowed with the best of fortune!" (41:34–35)

Jesus Said: Love Your Enemies

"But I say to you, love your enemies, bless anyone who curses you, do good to anyone who hates you, and pray for those who carry you away by force and persecute you, so that you may become sons of your Father who is in heaven, who causes His sun to shine upon the good and the wicked, and who pours down His rain upon the just and upon the unjust." (Matt. 5:44–48) "You must love your neighbors as yourself." (Mark 12:31)

The Golden Rule

The Golden Rule is a principle that appears in the Old Testament of the Bible in the form of specific verses and in Jesus' teachings. The Golden Rule states that people should treat others as they would like to be treated.

In the Old Testament

- Leviticus 19:18b: States that people should not take revenge or hold grudges against their relatives and love their neighbor as themselves. The Golden Rule appears positively in other Old Testament verses.

In Jesus' teachings

- Matthew 7:12: Jesus states that people should treat others as they would like to be treated and that this is the law.
- Luke 6:31: Jesus states that people should treat others as they would like to be treated.

The Golden Rule is a fundamental moral principle that applies to all people, regardless of their status or education. It's a way to live in love and generosity with others.

The Genetic Legacy of the Canaanites

Modern genetic research has shed light on ancestral connections between Jews and Arabs, challenging entrenched racial ideologies that fuel societal divisions. Studies reveal that cultural and societal conflicts may arise from constructed narratives rather than biological differences. Recognizing this shared heritage offers the potential to dismantle barriers that historically incited conflict, promoting a collective identity grounded in moral responsibility and mutual respect. The genetic legacy of the Canaanites reminds us that humanity is intrinsically interconnected. It advocates reconciliation and understanding in an often fragmented world.

All Peoples on Earth Will Be Blessed Through Abraham

It is worth repeating the third component of the original Abrahamic covenant with God: *I will make*

your name famous, and you will be a blessing. **All peoples on earth will be blessed through you."** *(Gen 12:4)* The third component, perhaps the most profound, is the universal promise of blessing. This promise positions Abraham not just as a recipient of God's favor but as a conduit of divine blessing for all humanity.

The Abrahamic Covenant extends into contemporary society, where it can serve as a bridge for interfaith reconciliation among Jewish, Christian, and Islamic communities. As adherents increasingly recognize their shared heritage, the potential exists for cultivating mutual respect and coexistence. By understanding the covenant as a relational pact that signifies God's ongoing engagement with humanity, members of these faith communities can illuminate their common values—such as faithfulness, ethical conduct, and justice. The recognition that all Abrahamic faiths stem from a common Divine source compels believers to work together toward reconciliation and healing. This is in a world fraught with sectarian divides. Indeed, "the children of Abraham" are called to forego rivalry and hostility in favor of embracing their shared mission to bless the world.

Jews Have a God-given Right to Live in Peace

Throughout history, Jews have faced persecution and violence. Upholding Islamic ideals of egalitarianism and humanitarianism, Jews have the right to live in peace and security.

"O Children of Israel! Remember those blessings of mine with which I graced you, and fulfill your promise unto Me, [then] I shall fulfill My promise unto you; and of Me, of Me stand in awe!" (2:40) "The people who [in the past] had been deemed utterly low, We gave as their heritage the eastern and western parts of the land that We had blessed. And [thus], thy Sustainer's good promise unto the children of Israel was realized because of their patience in adversity; whereas We utterly destroyed all that Pharaoh and his people had wrought, and all that they had built." (7:137) "And [remember] when you were told: 'Dwell in this land [Palestine] and eat of its food as you may desire; but say, 'Remove Thou from us the burden of our sins,' and enter the gate humbly. [Whereupon] We shall forgive you your sins [and] amply reward the doers of good." (7:161-162)

Palestine is spoken of as "blessed" because it was the land in which Abraham, Ishmael, Isaac, and Jacob lived, and because so many other prophets appeared there. The promise of God referred to here is given to the children of Israel through Moses.

The Promised Land and Equal Rights

The Quran asserts the rights of both Jews and Arabs to Palestine, emphasizing a shared heritage among the descendants of Isaac and Ishmael. Verses such as 2:40 affirm the legitimacy of Jewish claims to their ancestral lands, while simultaneously recognizing the Arab lineage stemming from Abraham's first son, Ishmael. The notion of a "promised land" thus transcends individual identity politics and underscores a collective Abrahamic heritage, fostering calls for mutual rights rather than heightened claims of supremacy. Muslims do not inherently oppose Jews or Israel; rather, they challenge its policies that perpetuate apartheid, subjugation, ethnic cleansing, and genocide of indigenous populations. The path toward peace in the Holy Land requires both Jews and indigenous peoples to embrace mutual respect and equal rights. All peoples on earth will finally be blessed through Abraham, fulfilling God's covenant.

www.ingramcontent.com/pod-product-compliance
Lightning Source LLC
Chambersburg PA
CBHW061729070526
44583CB00024B/3070